ECONOMIC WRITINGS OF JAMES PENNINGTON 1826-1840

LSE Scarce Tracts in Economics

XII

THE LONDON SCHOOL OF ECONOMICS SCARCE TRACTS IN ECONOMICS SERIES

1. Lectures on Political Economy, Mountifort Longfield, 1834
2. Three Lectures on Commerce and One on Absenteeism, Mountifort Longfield, 1835
3. The Graphic Representation of the Laws of Supply and Demand, and other Essays on Political Economy, Fleeming Jenkin, 1887
4. Grundzüge der Theorie des wirtschaftlichen Güterwerts, E. von Böhm-Bawerk, 1886
5. Tours in England and Wales, Arthur Young, 1784-1798
6. Industrial Combination, D H Macgregor, 1906
7. Protective and Preferential Import Duties, A C Pigou, 1906
8. Three Studies on The National Income, A. L. Bowley and Sir Josiah Stamp, 1919,1920 and 1927
9. A Study of Industrial Fluctuation, D. H Robertson, 1915
10. London Life in the Eighteenth Century, M Dorothy George, 1925
11. An Inquiry into the Currency Principle, Thomas Tooke, 1844
12. Economic Writings of James Pennington 1826-1840, Edited by R. S. Sayers, 1963

ECONOMIC WRITINGS OF JAMES PENNINGTON 1826-1840

Edited with an Essay on the Life and Work of James Pennington by

R. S. Sayers

Routledge
Taylor & Francis Group
LONDON AND NEW YORK

First published 1996 by Routledge/Thoemmes Press

2 Park Square, Milton Park, Abingdon, Oxfordshire OX14 4RN
605 Third Avenue, New York, NY 10017

Routledge is an imprint of the Taylor & Francis Group, an informa business

First issued in paperback 2020

British Library Cataloguing-in-Publication Data
A CIP record of this work is available from the British Library

ISBN 13: 978-1-138-86550-1 (pbk)
ISBN 13: 978-0-415-14396-7 (hbk)

CONTENTS

PREFATORY NOTE

THIS volume has grown from a decision by the London School of Economics to reprint the very scarce *Letter to Kirkman Finlay*. When, for the purpose of an introduction, I examined Pennington's other writings, it appeared that, after leaving aside items that were substantially reproduced with the *Letter*, the whole of Pennington's contribution to international trade and monetary controversy could be covered by a trifling expansion of the volume. Hence the inclusion of the papers of 1826 and 1838. The only publication not here in one way or another is *The Currency of the British Colonies*; this is a more narrowly technical volume, not of wide interest. All the printed works are listed, and their complex interrelationship analysed, in the bibliographical notes under the second sub-heading of the introductory essay.

I was invited to write an introduction as long ago as 1954; its appearance has been delayed by many distractions and I fear I may not now remember all who have helped me in the effort—not always successful—to find the story. Professor Jacob Viner, Professor Frank Whitson Fetter, Professor N. Gash, Mr. P. Sraffa, and Dr. L. S. Pressnell have all helped me from their rich stores of knowledge of the period. In many libraries and record repositories I have enjoyed eager and fruitful co-operation: especially the Guildhall Library (Mr. D. A. Dawe), C.R.O. India Records Section (Miss J. C. Lancaster), Public Record Office (Mr. E. K. Timings), British Museum Department of Manuscripts, Surrey Record Office, and the British Library of Economics and Political Science. The Goldsmiths' Librarian of the University of London has made the *Letter* available for reprinting; his assistants have helped me continually. For family information I owe much to Mr. and Mrs. R. Pennington, of London, Miss Ruth Pennington of Tadworth, and Mr. E. E. Smith of the Clapham Antiquarian Society. Miss Audrey Taylor has searched for some of the obscurer material, and Miss L. Malone has coped with a long succession of redrafts. To all these my thanks for much more than might be suggested by the slenderness of this volume.

R. S. S.
December, 1962

THE LIFE AND WORK OF JAMES PENNINGTON

PENNINGTON is a minor figure in English monetary history, winning a sentence here and a paragraph there, mostly as an appendage to Tooke or in the genesis of the Bank Charter Act of 1844. He wrote one of the clearest refutations of the notion that the possibility of prompt presentation is an adequate safeguard against the over-issue of paper money, and he originated the principle of currency regulation that, first as the Palmer Rule and then in the more rigorous form known as "The Currency Principle," became the accepted buttress of the principle of convertibility. He explained more exhaustively than hitherto, but did not originate, the view that bank deposits served as money. He showed, as early as 1838, how the Bank of England could force the market to conform with a discount rate of the Bank's own choice, though he did not develop the idea. He made an important contribution to the discussion on "sharing the gains of international trade." In all these matters he contributed by publication and, perhaps more influentially, in discussion at the Political Economy Club. He was intermittently an expert consultant for Government departments, first for the India Office, then for the Colonial Office, and finally for Peel and other Treasury Ministers.

All this has earned him little notice by posterity. Only writers on the development of monetary thought—Viner, Gregory, Robbins and Wood[1]—have mentioned him. Of these, Gregory alone, using Mallet's diary,[2] gives any portrayal of the man, and only Wood, who confines himself to purely monetary questions, pinpoints Pennington's

[1] J. Viner, *Studies in the Theory of International Trade* (?1937); T. E. Gregory, *An Introduction to Tooke and Newmarch's A History of Prices* (1928; L.S.E. Reprint, 1962); L. C. Robbins, *Robert Torrens and the Evolution of Classical Economics* (1958); E. Wood, *English Theories of Central Banking Control, 1819–1858* (1939).

[2] See below, pp. xxiii–xxiv.

contribution. Economic historians in general have left him alone, even when, like Clapham and Fay, they have been closely concerned with monetary developments. In the hundred years since Pennington's death there has been no systematic account of his activities. This emptiness may be partly ascribed to the lack of interest, in the first half of the twentieth century, in the Banking and Currency School controversies, a reason now over-ruled by the turn of monetary thought. The man himself has remained obscure partly because his only independent publication has been extremely scarce. Now that this scarcity is at last to be relieved by the present reprint, it is time to consider, on all the facts that can be ascertained, what manner of man James Pennington was, and what was his impact on the development of thought and on the current of events.

Antecedents and Early Career

James Pennington was born on 23rd February 1777, at Kendal in Westmorland, and died on 23rd March 1862 at Clapham. His life-span substantially coincided with that of Thomas Tooke, his close friend among economists, though not one to be identified with his mode of thought. When Pennington was born, the *Wealth of Nations* had only just left the printer's hands, and the Thirteen Colonies were fighting for the independence they had recently declared. When Pennington left his native Westmorland, Wordsworth had not yet put it on the literary map of England. The London in which he established himself was the London that heard the news of Trafalgar and of Waterloo. When he died, Darwin had lately found a new origin for the species, joint-stock companies were all the rage, and Overend and Gurney had only four years to run.

In Westmorland and Cumberland the Penningtons were in the eighteenth century a well-known group of families. One branch held a baronetcy, and an Irish barony, at Muncaster in Cumberland. Another, apparently descending from an outstanding Lord Mayor of London (1642–44), had joined the Society of Friends and early in the eighteenth century settled at Kendal in Westmorland. James's grandfather William was a millwright (Castle Mills, Kendal) who in 1738 married a local Irish lady, Bridget Hodgson. Their eleven children and twenty-two grandchildren formed part of the eighteenth century "explosion" of England's population, and in these two generations the family's history shows in microcosm how England prepared for the "wave of gadgets" that made the Industrial Revolution. Kendal had not room for all of them, and they migrated southward and eastward, taking their talents into varied occupations (watch-making, the law, medicine, and accounting among them) in London, Surrey, Oxfordshire, Sussex, Suffolk, Lincolnshire and Australia. Some stayed in Kendal; among these was William's fourth child, another William, who became a bookseller and printer, as well as being for many years Kendal's only architect; he was a Senior Alderman and eventually Mayor. In 1772 this second William married Agnes Wilson, a clockmaker's daughter bearing another north-country Quaker name. The third of their five children, born 1777, was one of the migrants: he was our James Pennington.[1]

James had the advantage of a grandfather whose ingenuity was subject of family legend; then as a boy such faculties as he had inherited were exposed to the influence of two quite extraordinary schoolmasters. A century earlier, the Society of Friends had established a school at Kendal, where in 1772 George Bewley became headmaster: "a man of superior mind and a good classic . . . proficient in the higher branches of mathematics."[2] In 1781 Bewley was joined by his cousin John Dalton, and it was probably soon after this that James Pennington was sent to the school. By the time Dalton left, in 1793, to become professor of mathematics and natural philosophy at Manchester (and to become famous for his Theory of the Atom), Pennington would have outgrown the schoolboy's

[1] For the early family history I have depended largely on a Family Tree (prepared in 1907) and other papers kindly shown to me by Mr. and Mrs. R. Pennington, of London, and an 1891 extract from a Kendal newspaper lent to me by Miss Ruth Pennington of Tadworth. The medical man was Dr. Pennington who served the Thorntons and other famous families at Clapham. (E. M. Forster, *Marianne Thornton*, London 1956, p. 123.)

[2] Sir E. T. Bewley, *The Bewleys of Cumberland* (1902).

clothes, but not, we may suppose, the training such teachers could give. Foreign exchange arithmetic was to hold no terrors for James Pennington.

From his schooldays in Kendal to his emergence in the commercial life of the City of London early in the new century there is a blank. In 1803 he became a Subscriber of Lloyd's, and remained so until 1832. In 1807 and 1808, with a Fenchurch Street address, he appeared as a contributor to the Royal Scottish Corporation (the Scottish Hospital founded by Charles II). On 30th November 1811 he married Mary Anne, daughter of John Harris of Clapham; at Clapham they lived for the rest of their lives.[1] Mrs. Pennington and their children were regular attendants at Clapham parish church, in a congregation that has a special place in history. In referring to this the eldest son (who became a Canon of Lincoln) makes no mention of his father,[2] but as the latter held a pew and was a Trustee of the Church's funds he had presumably moved away from any ancestral attachment to the Society of Friends.

When their first child was baptised (13th April 1813) James was described as a merchant and, although on later certificates of baptism he was sometimes "gentleman," by his own account[3] he continued in his "commercial pursuits" until 1832. At this date he was evidently an accountant of high standing, but neither the clues of addresses he used (Barge Yard, Bucklersbury, and Bridge St., Westminster) nor search of London Directories have revealed him in business under his own name; his claim to the attention of posterity was otherwise earned.

In 1832 Pennington was employed, in circumstances described below,[4] by the Board of Control for India and he thereupon abandoned his "commercial pursuits," whatever they were. As the employment was purely temporary and

[1] First at The Pavement, where they were near neighbours of the Macaulays. At some date between 1844 and 1851 they moved to 2 Nelson Terrace, now numbered 8 North Side, Clapham Common; this could be described as a good middle-class villa, quite small by Victorian standards.

[2] A. R. Pennington, *Recollections of Persons and Events* (London, 1895), pp. 5–12.

[3] *Complaint to Peel* (1844) (see below, p. xlii).

[4] Pp. xxiv–xxvi.

he had a large household to support,[1] Pennington would scarcely have taken this decisive step unless he was fairly well off. He was now, and for the rest of his life, "Mr. Pennington, political economist," as is written on the back of a portrait in the Marshall Library at Cambridge.[2] His first contribution to the subject had been made in 1826, and through the eighteen-thirties and 'forties his interventions in economic controversies appear to have been the chief interest of his life.

Pennington's Writings

In the following notes all Pennington's known published writings are included, together with the Memoranda he wrote for Huskisson. He used again and again, with very little alteration, the same material; in these notes I have shown the relationship of the various writings to each other. In making the selection for reprinting it has been my endeavour to minimize repetition whilst including, in one way or another, all controversial subjects on which Pennington made a real contribution. The following chronological and, I believe, comprehensive list may be of service to any who wish to trace the development of Pennington's thought more accurately than is possible by a study of only those items here reprinted.

Items marked * are included in the present volume.

* 1. *First Memorandum to Huskisson: Observations on the Private Banking Establishments of the Metropolis.*

13th February 1826. Not previously printed. Explains how deposits serve as money, and how their volume depends on the total of bank loans and securities. Not an original idea, but very clearly expounded; substantially

[1] All the seven children were then under 20. At the 1841 Census the household included five children and three servants.

[2] The portrait, an engaging crayon drawing dated 1833 by George Richmond, shows a handsome clean-shaven man, young for Pennington's 56 years, with a good crop of hair, turning white; the features are not perfectly symmetrical, and kindly eyes under dark strongly-curved eyebrows enforce the impression of a gentle yet not a yielding spirit. The identification with our James depends, however, entirely on the pencilling on the back of the frame, and it conflicts with the evidence of Richmond's papers, which show 40 guineas as received in October 1833 from "Robert R. Pennington" whom I have not been able to trace.

repeated by Pennington in his publications (Items 4, 5 and 11 below), but never more clearly developed than on this first occasion. The copy for this volume is taken from the British Museum (Add. MSS. 38761 ff. 201–210). The spelling, punctuation and lettering used in the present printing follows exactly that of this British Museum copy; it should be remembered that the British Museum document is itself a copy (cf. p. xviii below).

2. *Second Memorandum to Huskisson: Observations on the Coinage.*

16th May 1827. With Item 3, below, printed for private circulation ?1827. Explains technical arrangements of the gold standard and how maintenance of this standard is endangered by a paper currency. Except for the first four pages, and part of the fifth (these pages being concerned almost entirely with the reasons for choosing gold as the standard), this memorandum was reprinted, with trifling changes, on pp. 56–65 of the *Letter to Kirkman Finlay* (Item 9 below).

3. *Third Memorandum to Huskisson: On the Management of the Bank of England.*

23rd June 1827. With Item 2, above, printed for private circulation ?1827 (3 pages). The origin of the Currency Principle. Reprinted completely on pp. 12–14 of the *Letter to Kirkman Finlay* (Item 9 below).

4. Appendix No. 1 to Tooke's *Letter to Grenville*, 1829: *Paper communicated by Mr. Pennington* (11 pages). On the monetary nature and the importance of London bank deposits, repeating, with minor development, the *First Memorandum to Huskisson* (Item 1 above).

5. Appendix No. 1 to Torrens's *Letter to Melbourne*, 2nd Edition, 1837. *Paper by Mr. Pennington* (9 pages). An exact reprint of Item 4 above.

6. Appendix No. II to Torrens's *Letter to Melbourne*, 2nd Edition, 1837. *Paper communicated by Mr. Pennington* (5 pages). Expands slightly the exposition, given in Items 4 and 5 above, of the process of multiple expansion of bank deposits.

* 7. Appendix C to Vol. 2 of Tooke's *History of Prices*, 1838. *Letter addressed to the Author by James Pennington*

Esq. (10 pages). 10 April, 1838. Corrects a misunderstanding by Torrens. This arises from a paragraph near the end of Item 4, where illustrative figures show London banks as holding a one-fifth cash reserve against deposits. Torrens thereafter took Pennington as authority for the fixity, at one-fifth, of this reserve ratio, although in Items 4, 5 and 6 Pennington was even less explicit. Pennington now explains that he did not intend to imply a fixed ratio. He further develops the variability of bankers' operations. Mentions, with some scepticism, the idea of separating the Bank of England's deposit business from its note-issuing business.

8. In Vol. 3 of Tooke's *History of Prices* (1840): *Paper communicated by Mr. Pennington* (9 pages). Discusses the proposal for division of Bank of England into two departments, and is still sceptical of advantages of this proposal. Reproduced exactly, save for one change in the order of paragraphs, on pp. 91–102 of Item 9 below.[1]

* 9. *A Letter to Kirkman Finlay, Esq., on the Importation of Foreign Corn, and the Value of the Precious Metals in Different Countries. To which are added Observations on Money, and the Foreign Exchange.*

London: Simpkin Marshall & Co., and Pelham Richardson; Clapham, D. Batten, 1840 (114 pages). (See pp. xxx–xxxiv below.)

10. *The Currency of the British Colonies* (Anonymous), 1848. Published by H.M. Stationery Office (247 pages). A strictly factual account of the colonial currencies down to 1848, stressing the confusion of coinage; most valuable on the 1825 measures and their amendment 1838–44. An Appendix of official documents. (See p. xxix below.)

11. In *Supplement to Thoughts on a few subjects of Political Economy*, by John Cazenove, 1861. *Letter from Mr. Pennington on the London Banking System* (7 pages).

A somewhat developed version of Pennington's previous expositions of the power of the banks to create deposits, and of differences between London banks and country banks. Also notable for the idea that the Bank of England,

[1] The change is a reversal of the order of the two complete paragraphs on p. 100 of the *Letter to Kirkman Finlay.*

by its operations in securities or gold, can influence the rate of interest.

The Background of Thought

For the London in which Pennington launched these writings, the monetary scene was set by the establishment of the gold standard by "Peel's Bill" of 1819, the predominance of the Bank of England which enjoyed a monopoly (in England and Wales) of joint-stock banking and *de facto* a monopoly of note-issue in London, and a system of some hundreds of country banks, most of them new, loosely knit to the seventy London banks. In the first decade of the gold standard, the country experienced the extremes of boom and slump and late in 1825 a financial panic in which a large part of the banking structure broke down. In the wider economic field, the movements of prices were dominated by wide swings in the price of corn, imports of which were now always essential—though in greatly varying quantity—to provide the staple food of a surging population. It was inevitable that regulation of the monetary system and regulation of the import of corn should be—with certain macroeconomic questions of population and the distribution of wealth—the subjects of the most lively economic controversies. In all of these Pennington interested himself; all his known writings were on monetary questions or on the Corn Law.

Monetary controversy raged, almost continuously, round three questions. First, there were some who questioned the gold standard decision of 1819, and urged revision either by departure from gold or by devaluation.[1] These, despite the quality of the arguments some of them used, came to be regarded as almost a lunatic fringe, especially after 1833. The more general attitude was one of acceptance of the 1819 standard, but disappointment that the obligation of convertibility had apparently not precluded violent fluctuations of prices and production. Some found enough cause for the trouble in the weaknesses of the country banks, restricted in their legal powers and therefore in

[1] Some account of the discussion of this question is in R. S. Sayers, "The Question of the Standard, 1815–44" (*Economic History Suppl. of Economic Journal*, February 1935).

their growth by the Bank of England's monopoly. The most energetic propounder of this view was Thomas Joplin; Pennington did not develop it, although he was among the first to share (and expound more effectively than did Joplin himself) much of Joplin's theoretical basis.[1] The third stream of monetary debate, likewise starting from the assumption that the gold standard was right but that somehow convertibility of the notes was not enough to ensure its smooth working, was the Currency School *versus* Banking School debate. This stream of thought Pennington, it may be claimed, started when he responded, in 1827, to a request from Huskisson to develop a hint that had seemed to promise a solvent for the violent fluctuations that rocked the English monetary system.

Pennington's Memoranda for Huskisson

There is no evidence as to how Pennington's first contact with Ministers arose. It appears to have occurred in February 1826, when London, the country, and the Government were all smarting under the impact of the financial crisis of December 1825. Already before the crisis, banking reform had been in the air, a Government including Peel and Huskisson was not to be expected to stand idly by, and the Prime Minister (Liverpool) himself was ready with a plan of reform. From February onwards monetary questions were continually being debated in Parliament, and Huskisson was inevitably one of the three Ministers to bear the brunt of the battle.[2] "It was," Fay has told us,[3] "Huskisson's method, before making a big speech or taking important action . . . to call for memoranda." This does not mean that he called on Pennington for a memorandum—he may never have heard of him—but Huskisson would be known—for example, to Tooke—as a willing recipient of an expert memorandum.[4] Though not

[1] The best discussion of the common ground of Joplin and Pennington is in Elmer Wood, *English Theories of Central Banking Control*, 1819–1858 (Harvard, 1939), Chap. 2.

[2] N. Gash, *Mr. Secretary Peel* (London 1961), pp. 355–357.

[3] C. R. Fay, *Huskisson and his Age* (London 1951), p. 231.

[4] It is not impossible that J. D. Hume (whom Fay describes—*op. cit.*, p. 276 *et seq.*—as "Huskisson's trusted ally") would at this time have known Pennington, though Hume did not become a member of the Political Economy Club until 1834.

yet a member, Pennington was by this time known at the Political Economy Club, and there the problems now at issue in the Cabinet and in Parliament were discussed on 9th January and 6th February 1826, Pennington being a guest on the latter occasion.[1]

A few days later Pennington was writing the first memorandum he submitted to any Minister. The paper he later described as "containing observations on the private banking establishments of the metropolis,"[2] bears Pennington's date, Clapham, 13th February 1826, on the British Museum copy which is presumably that which Huskisson had had made for his own use before returning Pennington's original.[3] In this Memorandum, which is the first item reprinted in this collection, Pennington explained that deposits at the London banks served as money, just as did the notes of country banks; that loans by these banks created deposits; how the process of multiple expansion of deposits develops in a multi-bank system; and how the total of deposits is diminished by the contraction of bankers' loans in time of panic. This analysis was embodied in the appendix Pennington contributed to Tooke's *Letter to Grenville* (1829) and it became part of his regular stock-in-trade. Pennington was by no means the first to develop this theme, but use of it in the controversies of the succeeding quarter of a century probably had its source commonly in his work.

Meanwhile, the next step in Pennington's relations with Huskisson was taken on 16th May 1827, when Pennington, again without any request from Huskisson, sent some "Observations on the coinage." He had shown this paper to Tooke, but to no other expert;[4] it is on this fact that

[1] Neither Huskisson nor Hume was there (Political Economy Club *Minutes*, Vol. V, 1882, p. 77).

[2] Letter, Pennington to Huskisson, 16th May 1827, BM. Add. MSS. 38749, f. 262. No correspondence is attached to the memorandum, and from subsequent correspondence both with Huskisson and others we may deduce that Pennington did not even meet Huskisson.

[3] Huskisson's copy is Add. MSS. 38761, ff. 201–210, and bears the title, "Mr. Pennington on the London Banks"; for Huskisson's taking the copy, see his letter to Pennington, 1st June 1827, at 38749, f. 270.

[4] The statement is in a later letter: 23rd June 1827 (Add. MSS. 38749, f. 319b); Pennington was excepting "a neighbour in the country who takes a merely speculative interest in such matters."

it is possible to found a supposition that both this and the former communication to Huskisson had been suggested, or at least encouraged, by Tooke rather than anyone else. The latter part of the covering letter indicates the distance between the correspondents:

"I cannot but suppose, Sir, that communications upon subjects of this nature are not infrequently sent to you, which are deservedly thrown aside as useless and unimportant. Mine, it is not unlikely, will meet the same fate, and for the same reason. If so, the only request I have to make is that you will be so obliging as to return the papers to me at your convenience, or that you will have the goodness to destroy them.

"I have the honour to be,
with the greatest respect,
Sir,
Your very obedient and most humble servant,
James Pennington."

The paper sent with this letter did not suffer either of the fates suggested by its humble author; nevertheless, there is no copy among the Huskisson Papers. Possibly the original found its way to the Treasury, for it appears in the Welby Collection at the London School of Economics.[1] Its substance was reproduced in the *Letter to Kirkman Finlay* in 1840.[2] The purposes of the memorandum are (1) to explain the technical arrangements whereby the gold standard was established and maintained in England (an explanation that might have been beyond the Treasury "still inexpert in currency theory"[3]); and (2) to describe (rather than to explain) how the maintenance of a gold standard is endangered by the existence of a paper currency that experience has shown to be extremely difficult to control. The conclusion, after this parade of difficulties, was surprisingly encouraging. "The difficulty," wrote

[1] The Welby Collection on Banking and Currency. (Coll. R.I. in the British Library of Economics and Political Science.) The memorandum under reference is on ff. 221–225. (R. E. (later Baron) Welby entered the Treasury in 1856 and was Permanent Secretary 1885–94.)

[2] See *Advertisement* on the back of the title-page; and pp. 56–65 of the pamphlet.

[3] The quotation is from H. A. Shannon, in *I.M.F. Staff Papers*, April 1951, p. 338.

Pennington, ". . . is not insuperable. It is possible to regulate an extensive paper circulation . . . to render its contraction and expansion . . . subject to the same Law as that which determines the expansion and contraction of a currency wholly and exclusively metallic." Here indeed was the hint of a panacea.

Returning the paper to Pennington (after taking a copy), Huskisson took the hint, and now for the first time invited a further contribution. The invitation was explained with some care; it was a letter Pennington did not forget:[1]

"I perceive that towards the end of your Paper upon Coinage, you state an opinion that means may be found of preventing those alternations of excitement and depression which have been attended with such alarming consequences to this Country. This, for a long time, has appeared to me to be one of the most important matters which can engage the attention of the Legislature and the Councils of the Country. The subject is certainly intricate and complicated, but the too great facility of expansion at one time, and the too rapid contraction of paper credit (I speak of it in the largest sense) at another, is unquestionably an evil of the greatest magnitude. To devise a safe remedy, and to apply it when found, are not easy tasks in the present artificial state of the Country, and with a due regard to all the great interests which are at stake.

"Upon this subject I am anxious to collect as much as possible Information and suggestions from others who have turned their attention to it; and as it is obvious that you have, I hope you will excuse the liberty I now take of stating that it would be a great satisfaction to me to be favoured with your written opinions upon this point; or if you should not feel disposed to commit them to writing, that you will allow me, when I have leisure for the purpose, to see you with a reference to those opinions."[2]

It was this invitation—Huskisson as usual calling for a memorandum[3]—that in 1827 evoked the first known formulation of that principle for regulating the note issue

[1] He used quotation from it as a conclusion for his pamphlet in 1840 (*Letter to Kirkman Finlay*, p. 114).

[2] BM. Add. MSS. 38749, f. 270b.

[3] Cf. above, p. xvii.

which later became famous as "The Currency Principle."[1] To secure the advantages of a paper currency consistently with complete stability of its value in terms of gold, some simple regulation of the issue of notes would be ideal. If the Bank of England were the only issuer of paper money, or if the London and country banks were in all cases directly and immediately controlled by the Bank, all would be very simple: the Bank of England would be required to keep its securities fixed in total amount. The conditions were, however, of great importance, as might be judged from Pennington's previous memoranda; moreover, there was the treatment of the deposits at the Bank of England itself to be considered, and this, Pennington showed, was no straightforward problem. He concluded with a further reference to the relevance of bank deposits generally: "to regulate them properly will be no easy task." This was anything but a blueprint for legislation, and it was only after Pennington's massive qualifications had been, in one way or another, thrust aside that the simple Currency Principle—the principle of the fixed fiduciary issue—did form the basis of legislation in 1844. Pennington had, in short, failed to give Huskisson the practical advice seemingly promised in the conclusion of his second memorandum, and he must have realized that this was so. Indeed, he himself emphasized all the difficulties; "A material point will however have been gained when the nature of the evil is fully and distinctly perceived and understood." Others could not take so detached a view, and in the next few years the Bank of England began experimenting with that form of

[1] J. Viner (*Studies in the Theory of International Trade* (1937), says (p. 224) "Pennington, a confidential adviser of the Treasury on currency matters, had recommended the same rule in a Memorandum to Huskisson, then Chancellor of the Exchequer"; this, it will be appreciated from the story as told above, over-states Pennington's position at this time. Huskisson was never at the Exchequer, but was at the time President of the Board of Trade; the letter quoted above, however, shows how seriously he took the Government's responsibilities for regulation of the monetary system. According to Tooke (*History of Prices*, iv. 166) the term "Currency Principle" was first used in 1840. Elmer Wood (*English Theories of Central Banking Control*, Harvard, 1939, p. 111) finds the term "The Principle of Currency" being used by Ward in the 1832 inquiry; Ward was, however, using this term (e.g. in Qus. 2033, 2034 and 2035) for the Ricardian principle that an influx of gold should be followed by an increase in the issue of notes, not for the more refined rule of keeping the securities unchanged in amount.

the Currency Principle which came to be known as the Palmer Rule.[1]

What Huskisson felt about Pennington's academic exercise does not appear; there is no trace of any further correspondence between them, and it seems unlikely that they had any important later contact. After the legislation of 1826 Ministers were glad enough to let monetary matters run; Huskisson, like other Ministers,[2] had other problems on his mind, and through the remaining three years before his death he was in indifferent health and moved less outside his own circle, a circle in which the bookseller's son from Kendal had no natural place.[3]

Pennington at the Political Economy Club

It was four years before Pennington was again to be thought useful to Ministers; and it was during these years that he became a very active member of the Political Economy Club. He had already been eight times a guest at the Club in 1824–28,[4] and in 1828, on the introduction of Tooke,[5] he was elected to membership. Ricardo was already dead—there is no evidence that Pennington ever had any contact with him[6]—but among the members at

[1] The exact date of the Bank's adoption of the Palmer Rule cannot be established. The Court of Directors appointed a Select Committee in December 1830. Its Report advocated the Rule, though not in unquestioned terms. There is in the Bank no trace of adoption of the Report, but certain answers (Qus. 84, 85 and 269) by Palmer to the Committee on the Bank Charter in 1832 (P.P. Sess. 1831–32 (722) Vol. 6) are open to the interpretation that the Rule had been adopted in 1830 or even a little earlier. Certainly it was, in 1832 and afterwards, regarded as established practice in 1832. The antecedents of the Rule are discussed in J. K. Horsefield, *The Bank and its Treasure* (*Economica*, May 1940; reprinted in Ashton and Sayers, *Papers in English Monetary History*, Oxford, 1953), but Horsefield had no access to the Bank of England's records used in this note.

[2] Huskisson resigned in May 1828 and did not again hold office.

[3] In that ebullient study of sunshine and shadows, *Huskisson and his Age*, C. R. Fay did not mention Pennington at all. This is not absolutely conclusive—Fay must, from his study of the Huskisson Papers, have known of Pennington—but I judge that, if there had been any significant contact beyond that related here, Fay would have found in Pennington just the kind of character he would have delighted to chase down.

[4] *Political Economy Club Minutes*, Vol. V, 1882.

[5] *Ibid.*

[6] The *D.N.B.* puts Pennington's attraction of "the favourable notice of Huskisson, Ricardo and Tooke" as after 1832, long after both Huskisson and Ricardo were dead. Ricardo was dead before Pennington first went as a guest to the Club; there is no mention of Pennington in Ricardo's published correspondence (Sraffa edition).

the time of his election were Malthus, James Mill, G. W. Norman, Sir H. Parnell, Tooke, Torrens and Senior. Others who became members during Pennington's most active period in the Club (1828–35) were McCulloch, Horsley Palmer, S. J. Loyd (Lord Overstone), J. D. Hume, Edwin Chadwick and Thomas Hyde Villiers.[1]

During these years the questions formally discussed in the Club reflected the interests of the economists in the broad questions of national policy: public finance, money, international trade, macroeconomic questions of distribution, and problems of measurement. Of the questions opened by Pennington himself (six in this active period, and two in later years) three were monetary, two were on foreign trade, and the other three a miscellany of macroeconomic subjects. On other occasions when Mallet or some other diarist noted Pennington's participation, four were on monetary questions, one on foreign trade, and one on taxation. Pennington was particularly prominent in discussions on the Corn Laws; in April 1832 he developed his view (later to be published in his *Letter to Kirkman Finlay*) that the advantage of free importation would be much less than was commonly asserted,[2] and at the big meeting of the Club on 5th February 1846—when he was 69 and had become much less active in its proceedings—he spoke in support of Peel's measures. His other great subject was the currency. When the question of a Government monopoly of note issue was discussed, and there were great differences of opinion, Pennington, with Loyd and Tooke, urged a restriction of the Bank of England to the business of note issue on Ricardian lines; he seems to have modified this a month later, when he wanted "a fixed amount of notes" to be issued by "a Government Commission."

Mallet's comments show that Pennington had outstanding analytical ability: "Mr. Pennington has considerable powers of abstraction, and is a true disciple of the analytical school; and he began by expressing his fears—for he is a

[1] Political Economy Club *Centenary Volume* (London 1921) (referred to below as P.E.C.) is the main source for this and the following two paragraphs.

[2] P.E.C., p. 233.

very modest man—that as the discussions of the Society had of late turned much upon practical subjects, he might be deemed a little tedious, and perhaps not quite intelligible."[1] His manner of speaking did not help: "Pennington is a man who will go on in the same monotonous tone through all the mazes of the most elaborate and complicated argument. He is more like Babbage's machine for working out logarithms than anything else I know, incapable of any mistake in the connection and proper series of his ideas, but impossible to follow unless you could put your understanding in the same box."[2] After 1835 he seems to have been less active at the Club, and when he spoke in 1846 he is reported to have been indistinct.[3] But he remained a member long enough to see William Newmarch into the Club before he resigned in 1856.

Pennington as a Consultant for Ministers and Government Departments, 1832–1841

The employment of Pennington by the India Office had its origin in the enquiries that preceded the termination of the trading business of the East India Company. "It was a wish often and strongly expressed by the Committee of 1831[4] that in order to ascertain whether the objections which had been raised, both in and out of Parliament, to the system on which the public accounts of the company had been framed, were or were not well founded, some person thoroughly conversant with accounts, and unconnected either with the company or the Board, should be employed to examine the accounts in all their bearings. . . ."[5] It was "at the recommendation of the President" (Charles

[1] P.E.C., p. 260. The question (1st May 1834) was on the incidence of import duties.

[2] P.E.C., p. 260. The question was of the depreciation of a gold currency. Cf. (p. 226) his insistence on "the six different senses" of a fall and rise of wages, "which ought all to be kept *distinct from each other*."

[3] But this was by a Frenchman (P.E.C., p. 294).

[4] This would be the Select Committee (of the H. of C.) "on the present state of the Affairs of the East India Company, and on the state of the trade between Great Britain, the East Indies and China." (Sess. 1831.)

[5] Minute of the Board of Commissioners for the Affairs of India, 30th January 1832 (*Minutes*, 1815–46, ff. 367–369). The Minute Books and Letter Books referred to in these four paragraphs are in the India Office Records at the Commonwealth Relations Office, London.

Grant)[1] that the Board on 30th January 1832 appointed Pennington to this task, "a gentleman who from his talents, and the peculiar nature of his attainments, appears eminently qualified. . . ." In connection with this appointment, Auber, then Secretary of the East India Company, subsequently referred to Pennington as a professional accountant.[2] Remuneration was to be at the rate of £100 a month for the first three months, and for any further period at £1000 per annum. On 1st December 1833, the Board authorized payment of £967 to Pennington, the President "having employed Mr. Pennington in a variety of enquiries and calculations. . . ."[3] This payment was presumably additional to what had been covered by the Minute of 30th January 1832.

Meanwhile there had been another resolution on 28th November 1833.[4] Pennington was to "attend upon" the Board "during the winding up of the Company's commercial business." This involved "a pecuniary trust of great delicacy and importance. . . . Adverting to the responsible nature of Mr. Pennington's duties, to his peculiar qualifications for the office to which he is now appointed, to the service which he has already rendered to the Board, to his sacrifice of his professional[5] business, to the inadequate compensation which he has received for those services and sacrifices, and to the great pecuniary trust . . . his allowances should be placed upon a liberal footing. . . ." He was to receive £1500 p.a., "to include the stipend of a Clerk, if he should find it necessary to employ one."[6] There was provision for review in April 1837 if continuation beyond that date should be required.[7]

[1] In his *Complaint to Peel* (see below, p. xli) Pennington said that it was "at the request of the late Mr. Hyde Villiers, then Secretary to the India Board." T. H. Villiers (1801–32) was a friend of J. S. Mill (certainly in 1825), and a member of the Political Economy Club (1831–32); heavy work at the India Office is supposed to have contributed to his death on 3rd December 1832.

[2] P. Auber, *The Rise and Progress of the British Power in India*, Vol. 2, p. 680.

[3] *Minutes*, 1815–46, ff. 382–3.

[4] *Minutes*, 1815–46, ff. 375–8.

[5] The word "professional" is not clear; it might conceivably be "personal."

[6] There is no evidence that he did employ a clerk, and he later, when writing to Peel (see below, p. xli) stated his remuneration simply as "£1500 p.a."

[7] Pennington later argued that this implied longer employment than the 16 months that eventuated.

This was all under Grant's Presidency of the Board of Control.[1] When Lord Ellenborough succeeded him (in Peel's first Ministry, December 1834), the new broom quickly determined that Pennington was unnecessary, having regard to recent reinforcement of the accounting side of the Office. It looks as though the matter was discussed informally almost immediately after the change of Ministry, and on 22nd January 1835, it was the subject of formal Minute by the Board.[2] The appointment was to terminate at 25th March, and Pennington was to receive a gratuity of £500, in addition to the salary to that date. The gratuity was in acknowledgement of "the disappointment you will experience, in consequence of the early termination of your employment."[3] Pennington was disgruntled, and remained so, at least until 1844. He appealed to Ellenborough, who replied rather sharply.[4] Pennington was not to be put off; he wrote again and again. After another change of Ministry (Hobhouse succeeding Ellenborough) Pennington proposed arbitration;[5] when he appealed against refusal of this, Pennington was told that "it would not answer any purpose beneficial to you that the controversy should be continued with the present Board."[6] But Pennington persisted, and eventually, after referring to the Treasury, the India Board paid a further £1000, so making the gratuity equal to one year's salary.[7]

This closed the episode. When, in 1844, Pennington wrote his long complaint to Peel,[8] he stated the facts of this employment correctly, but he did not mention that he had

[1] When he went out of office, Grant pointedly included Pennington in his message of praise to the staff of the office (*Minutes*, f. 435). Grant, being "a wretched man of business" (N. Gash, *Mr. Secretary Peel*, London 1961, p. 367), was no doubt glad of a helper whose forte was the sorting out of facts.

[2] The Minute refers to previous communication by Ellenborough to Pennington (*Minutes*, 1815–46, ff. 439–41).

[3] Letter, W. M. Praed to J. Pennington, 23rd January 1835 (*Letter Book*, Vol. 11, 1833–37, f. 126).

[4] *Letter Book*, Vol. 11, 1833–37.

[5] Letter, J. C. Hobhouse to J. Pennington, 29th May 1835 (*Letter Book*, Vol. 11, 1833–37, f. 164).

[6] Letter, R. V. Smith to J. Pennington, 20th June 1835, *ibid.*, f. 169.

[7] *Letter Book*, Vol. 11, 1833–37, ff. 211–13 and 244–5; and *Minute Book*, f. 481.

[8] See below, p. xli.

received a gratuity of £1500. He merely wrote of being "thrown back upon my own weakened resources." He claimed that his report was "satisfactory to, and met with the approbation of, not only the Board of Control, but likewise of the Parliamentary Committee then sitting."[1] This is consistent with the attitude of Grant[2] and the tone of the correspondence generally; every indication is that he gave complete satisfaction, and that termination was simply due to the completion of specific tasks and the strengthening of the official staff for continuing tasks.

In 1837 the Colonial Office and the Treasury were faced with urgent problems on the currencies of the West Indian colonies.[3] Troop commanders and the Commissariat were complaining of the insufficiency and inconveniences of the coinage, and it was anticipated that the emancipation of the slaves, by adding greatly to the small wage payments and other money transactions to be effected, would aggravate these difficulties.[4] According to Pennington himself,[5] he was called in "at the suggestion of Lord Glenelg, then Secretary of State for the Colonies." This Lord Glenelg was the Charles Grant who, as President of the India Board, had been pleased with Pennington's work in 1831–32. Taking the Colonial Office in Melbourne's second Cabinet (April 1835), it had fallen to his lot to introduce the Bill for abolition of slavery in the West Indies, a task that must have been singularly gratifying to a member of the Clapham Sect.[6] The Treasury Minute of 22nd September 1837[7] selected Mr. James Pennington for investigation of the problem, he being "a party conversant with questions of this description and scientifically acquainted with the

[1] This report referred to his first task (under the Minute of 30th January 1832).

[2] See above, p. xxvi, fn. 1.

[3] The Colonial Office papers referred to in this section are at the P.R.O., under ref. CO 318-134, in Box T.1. 3624, Parts I and II, and in *West Indian Miscellany*, 1838, Vol. 3.

[4] Pennington's second Report, 17th August 1838 (No. 17850.X).

[5] *Complaint to Peel.*

[6] A. T. Embree, *Charles Grant and British Rule in India* (London, 1962), p. 272. The Charles Grant who is the subject of Embree's book was the father of Lord Glenelg. See also H. Morris, *Life of Charles Grant* (London 1904), and M. Hennell, *John Venn and the Clapham Sect* (London, 1958).

[7] P.R.O., T.29.393, ff. 333–334.

principles by which the Currency and Circulatory medium of this Country and of other States are regulated and governed"; he was "a Gentleman peculiarly qualified by his knowledge and experience." All the relevant papers received from the colonies were thereupon referred to him; the first batch was followed by others, but there does not appear to have been any further formal Minute. Pennington made his first Report apparently in March 1838; there is no copy in the public records. His Second (and apparently final) Report was dated 17th August 1838.[1] It described the origin, and the urgency, of the problem. It contained detailed factual material, clearly set out, leading to the conclusion that the source of trouble was not in the principles of the ordinances of 1825 (which now regulated the West Indian and other colonial currencies),[2] but in the ratios fixed between the various coins.[3]

According to Robert Chalmers,[4] a Committee of the Privy Council was appointed in 1838 to hold an enquiry, "and the root of the evil was shown by Mr. James Pennington to be the erroneous rating of the dollar, according to the 'Mint Price' of 5s. 2d. per ounce standard, instead of according to the market price (then 5s.)." No trace of this Committee has survived, but it may be presumed that the Pennington Reports referred to above are in effect papers for this Committee.

The result was that the Order in Council of 1825 was revoked, and a new Order in Council was made on 14th September 1838, under which the coins could be tendered at appropriate values. Parallel reforms were promulgated in 1843–44 in other parts of the world, and it was not until new problems were encountered in the silver areas of the East that Pennington's revamping of the system of 1825 proved inadequate.[5] On remuneration for these and

[1] No. 17850.X in Box T.1. 3624, Part 1.

[2] For the historical background, the arrangements made in 1825 and experience of them, see the important article "*Evolution of the Colonial Exchange Standard*" by H. A. Shannon (*I.M.F. Staff Papers*, April 1951, pp. 334–339).

[3] Cf. Pennington's account in his *The Currency of the British Colonies* (London, 1848), p. 36, on which see below, p. xxix.

[4] In his *History of Currency in the British Colonies* (London, 1893) which was based on official records. See Preface and pp. 26–27 for this episode.

[5] Chalmers, *op. cit.*, pp. 29–30.

occasional later consultations[1] there is no evidence beyond that from Pennington himself: in 1844[2] he stated that it consisted "at first of small sums occasionally paid to me, and . . . latterly . . . quarterly payments, from the Special Service Fund at the rate of £500 per annum." It seems likely that these payments continued after 1844: certainly covering the preparation of his book.

This book was *The Currency of the British Colonies*, which appeared anonymously as an official publication, in 1848.[3] In this Pennington put together for official use factual material on colonial currencies, including much detail about the metallic equivalence of various coins. He explained how the over-valuation of gold had gradually led to a scarcity of coin, why the 1825 measures failed, and how the 1838–44 measures remedied the situation. Although these last measures were essentially his own work, the whole story is told completely impersonally. When Chalmers extended the story 45 years later, he remarked that Pennington's work was especially valuable on the remedial legislation of which he was the author, but that his researches into earlier history had been narrowly limited. There is no indication of any kind that Pennington ever visited the colonies. The book shows, as one would expect, facility in using the relevant Ricardian analysis (Gresham's Law is prominent, though not mentioned by this name), but it is first-rate technical work rather than a path-breaking advance of monetary thought.

This episode of consultation on colonial currencies seems to have established Pennington as, in a humble degree, a regular source of technical advice for Government departments when questions of this kind arose. When, in 1839, Spring-Rice was Chancellor of the Exchequer, the problem of wear on the gold coinage, entailing the question whether tax collectors and others should refuse light coins, became acute, and the Bank of England and the Mint reported to

[1] E.g. Box T.1. 3624 Part I (28th April 1840) and Part II (No. 1259, 14th January, 1839).

[2] In his *Complaint to Peel*.

[3] The copy in the Goldsmiths Library, University of London, is inscribed "The Right H'ble Sir Robert Peel Bart., with Mr. Pennington's respectful compliments."

the Chancellor on the subject. The Chancellor thereupon referred all the papers to Pennington, who returned a very learned Memorandum entitled *Memorandum on the State of the Gold Coin.*[1] After recounting the history of the coinage from early times and using Ricardian analysis on the distribution of the precious metals, Pennington got to grips with the problem of the moment and advised that the prevalence of light coin could be stamped out by the tax collectors' insisting on weighing all gold coin tendered to them and refusing the light coin, which would then be sold for its bullion value to the Bank of England. When Baring shortly afterwards succeeded Spring-Rice at the Exchequer, Pennington sent a copy to him; then again, on Goulburn's succession in 1841, Pennington sent a copy to the Treasury for Goulburn. "It may perhaps," wrote Pennington in his usual style, "be regarded as of little worth—but the subject to which it relates is a matter of great practical importance and has an important bearing on many of the great questions which will I apprehend ere long be pressed on the consideration of Government." Goulburn was not impressed: "There is nothing in this," he pencilled on the bundle, and tucked it away.

The Letter to Kirkman Finlay

Goulburn's attitude might easily have meant an end to Pennington's career as consultant, but the great question of how the principle of convertibility might be effectively reinforced was now coming to a head, and this was a subject on which Pennington had already made himself heard in the great world. He had in fact, in the year previously to his submission to Goulburn, published a pamphlet that was at once a contribution to the Corn Laws debate and an assemblage of some of his more important writings bearing on the monetary debate: the two debates that were to

[1] The Memo and the correspondence relating to it are among the Goulburn Papers at the Surrey Record Office, Kingston-on-Thames (Acc. 319, Box II/13). T. Spring-Rice (later Lord Monteagle) was a member of the Political Economy Club. He was succeeded as Chancellor of the Exchequer by F. T. Baring in August 1839; Goulburn followed in September 1841.

Pennington included a long quotation from this Memorandum in the *Note* he wrote for Peel on 25th April 1844 (see below, p. xxxvii).

dominate the 'forties. This pamphlet is *A Letter to Kirkman Finlay, Esq., on the Importation of Foreign Corn, to which are added Observations on Money, and the Foreign Exchange*. This has become extremely scarce, and is now reprinted for (I believe) the first time.

Much of this pamphlet had been in print before, in one place or another. The new part of it was the *Letter*, covering pp. 5–50; this, Pennington tells us in the "Advertisement" on the back of the title-page, was written in the early part of 1839. As there is a gap of over a year between this date and that of the Advertisement, it may be presumed that Pennington did actually send this paper as a letter to Kirkman Finlay, with whom we know him to have been in touch.[1] The remainder (pp. 51–114) consists of the *Observations*. Of these, Pennington tells us in the Advertisement, "Much of what relates to coinage was submitted to the late Mr. Huskisson, in the year 1827. The memorandum on the management of the Bank of England was drawn up at his request." In fact substantially all of this part of the pamphlet was old material,[2] and the amendments are trivial. It seems probable that Pennington's main object was the publication of his new work, a contribution to the theory of international trade directly relevant to the Corn Law controversy, and that he merely made use of the opportunity this afforded for wider circulation of former writings that were highly relevant to the monetary controversy simultaneously raging. In fact the circulation of the pamphlet, if one is to judge by its present scarcity, must have been extraordinarily small, and posterity has come to know of Pennington rather through the appendices he contributed to Tooke's widely circulated volumes.

In the *Letter* itself (pp. 5–50) it looks as though Pennington's approach was through the relationship between corn prices, as influenced by conditions special to the trade in corn, and the general level of prices, as influenced by the supply of money. By using the analysis thus developed he sought to forecast *how greatly* the price of corn would be

[1] Letter, Pennington to Peel, 12th April 1847, BM. Add. MSS. 40598, f. 160.

[2] For the writings in which it had previously appeared, see p. xiv above.

affected by reduction of the import duties on corn. He started from a strictly Ricardian comparative costs analysis, but he did not find here a complete answer to the questions in his mind. It was at one time supposed that Pennington corrected an error in Ricardo. This, as Sraffa showed,[1] is not so: Ricardo made no error, but Pennington took the subject further. He seems, says Viner,[2] "to have been the first explicitly to point out in print that the comparative costs set maximum and minimum rates for the terms of trade, and that within these limits the operation of reciprocal demand could fix the terms of trade at any point." J. S. Mill did not publish his treatment of the subject until 1844 (*Essays on some unsettled questions*),[3] but he had written in 1829 and 1830, and it is not unlikely that he and Pennington (both members of the Political Economy Club) had heard each other speak on the point. If Mill was indeed the originator, posterity has done him justice, in that it was from Mill's "exposition in the Essays, repeated and developed in the Principles . . . that later economists took over the doctrine."[4] But it remains true that Pennington's treatment, the first to be published, is elegant, and the practical conclusion Pennington drew from it—that the relative cheapening of corn after abolition of the import duty might not be so very great—looks well in the light of the historic lag of a quarter of a century between the Repeal of the Corn Laws and the really big effect.

Precisely why this pamphlet was addressed to Kirkman Finlay is not known. Finlay (1772–1842) was a famous Lord Provost of Glasgow (1812), an energetic merchant who had given new life to his city's commerce at the end of the eighteenth century, and a cotton manufacturer who advised Gladstone on the early Factory Acts.[5] As a member

[1] P. Sraffa, "An alleged correction of Ricardo," *Quarterly Journal of Economics*, XLIV (1929–30), pp. 439–44.

[2] *Studies in the Theory of International Trade*, p. 477. The relevant passage in Pennington is on pp. 32–41 of the *Letter*.

[3] Reprinted in the present L.S.E. series, No. 7 (1948).

[4] Viner, *op. cit.*, p. 447, which these three sentences follow closely.

[5] Most of what is known about Kirkman Finlay is to be found in an anonymous article, "Kirkman Finlay: Merchant, Manufacturer and Mentor," in the *Three Banks Review*, March 1957. C. R. Fay (*Huskisson and his Age*, pp. 370–371) describes Finlay as the "Scottish *alter ego*" of John Gladstone, the statesman's father.

of Parliament he was notable for his speeches on economic subjects; he was prominent in the agitation which in 1826 saved the Scottish one-pound note, and in the same year in a newspaper correspondence he argued strongly against devaluation.[1] There is evidence, in the Minute Books of the Royal Bank of Scotland of which he was an Extraordinary Director, that in 1836 Finlay had a correspondent in the London money market;[2] conceivably this was Pennington, or Pennington may, as a member of Lloyd's have been concerned in the insurance of Finlay cargoes. Finlay's interest in the Corn Law question was, in any case, well-known, for his protectionist stand in this, contrasting with his Free Trade attitude in other contexts, had angered Glasgow.

There is no trace of any reaction from Kirkman Finlay, except a statement by Pennington himself that Finlay had told him of his intention to send copies of the pamphlet to Gladstone and Peel.[3] There was, in 1841, a brief pamphlet of comment, by Holt Mackenzie: *Notes addressed to Mr. Pennington on his Pamphlet on the Importation of Foreign Corn.*[4] This is entirely confined to corn trade questions: the upshot is that as little was known about the elasticity of supply of corn from other countries, forecasts of a low price following abolition of the duties had little basis. The "Advertisement" included[5] a note, evidently written by Pennington himself.[6] "If Mr. Pennington should hereafter publish a second edition of his pamphlet on the Importation of foreign corn, it is his intention to add to it some explanatory remarks on the points discussed. He does not, however, deem it right, on that account, to withhold Mr. Mackenzie's Notes from the public, at the present moment." Pennington did not, in the event,

[1] This last fact is not in the above cited article, but is mentioned on p. 27 of R. Cruttwell, *The System of Country Banking Defended* (London, 1828). Cruttwell states the date of the letter as 25th December 1826, but I have not been able to trace it.

[2] The Royal Bank of Scotland kindly provided me with an extract from the Minutes of their Court of Directors, 23rd November 1836.

[3] Letter, Pennington to Peel, 12th April 1847. BM. Add. MSS. 40598, f. 160.

[4] London: Simpkin Marshall & Co. and Pelham Richardson, 1841.

[5] On the back of the title-page.

[6] Dated "Clapham Common, June 10, 1841."

publish a second edition, and his contribution to all the discussions, both on the monetary system and on the Corn Laws, seems to have been overshadowed by the works of J. S. Mill and others through the remainder of the century.

Pennington as Adviser to Peel and other Ministers, on the Bank Charter Act of 1844 and other Monetary Questions

The attraction of a fixed fiduciary issue derives, as we have seen, from Pennington's third Memorandum to Huskisson, where it is suggested, in a highly theoretical way, that the supply of money would be sufficiently regulated if the Bank of England held the total of securities unchanged. This became known as the Palmer Rule, from its exposition by Horsley Palmer in Evidence to the 1832 Committee[1] as the recently established practice of the Bank, then under his governorship. In 1827, however, Pennington had emphasized the various complications that made the theory inadequate as a guide to practice. Among these complications was the deposit business, itself not a single homogeneous factor, of the Bank of England. The one important development of thought among the writers later known as the Currency School was their attempt, during the 1830's, to deal with this particular complication, and so evolve what they regarded as a practical rule, by proposing separation of the business of note-issue from the banking business of the Bank of England. This development of thought was at first resisted by Pennington, but he later became one of its staunchest supporters and remained so after the Bank Charter Act of 1844 had given statutory effect to the idea.

The change in his position came at some date between 1839 and 1844, and appears[2] to have been prompted by study of the evidence given by the Bank to the Committee on Banks of Issue (1840–41). His position in 1839, before the change, is shown in the *Paper* he wrote in that year,

[1] Bank of England Charter. Cttee of Secrecy. 1831–32. See especially Qus. 84 and 85.

[2] Letter to C. Wood. Peel Papers, 13th June 1844, BM. Add. MSS. 40546, ff. 322–5.

which was printed as part of Chapter V of Tooke's third volume, published in 1840.[1] He used almost identical phrases in the *Observations* which were published with the *Letter to Kirkman Finlay*; these may be presumed to represent his views in June 1840.[2] In both these publications Pennington refers to the alleged insufficiency of the Palmer Rule, and to the proposals now being made for separation of the departments, with a fixed amount of securities in the "circulating department" (i.e. a fixed fiduciary issue of notes, plus pound for pound issue against gold) and conduct of the "deposit department" "on the ordinary principles which are observed by the London bankers." He argued (correctly) that, if the principle of fixed fiduciary issue were adopted, the separation of departments would be an irrelevant frill. He went on to argue that in either case, a fixed fiduciary issue would cause the public to be "exposed to very great alternations of comparative ease and difficulty in the operations of the money market." Characteristically, Pennington did not conclude with explicit condemnation of the Currency School's proposals, but this reference to "very great alternations," read in the light of his repeated references to "those alternations of excitement and depression" as the evils he was seeking to overcome,[3] can only be interpreted as rejection of the principle of the fixed fiduciary issue as dangerous and of separation of the departments as irrelevant. He concluded without any alternative plan but with the warning that "the utmost caution will be necessary in endeavouring to remedy those defects" and with a repetition of Huskisson's judgement (1827) that "to devise a safe remedy . . . will be no easy task."[4]

When he wrote to Charles Wood (on monetary matters Peel's strong supporter in the House of Commons) on 11th

[1] *A History of Prices, and of the State of the Circulation, in* 1838 *and* 1839 . . . London, 1840 (generally referred to as the third volume of Tooke's *History of Prices*).

[2] Cf. above, p. xxxi. The *Letter* itself was written early in 1839, but the *Observations* were a revision of the 1827 Memoranda for Huskisson, and the date June 1840 is that of Pennington's note in the "Advertisement."

[3] E.g. in the *Memorandum* to Huskisson, 16th May 1827. (The second of the three Memos. to Huskisson referred to on pp. xiii–xiv above.)

[4] *Letter*, p. 114.

June 1844,[1] Pennington said that, when he wrote the *Paper* printed in Tooke's third volume, he had not been "acquainted with the working of the Bank of England, as it has since been disclosed in the Appendix to the Report on Banks of Issue."[2] He now (1844) believed that, had the Currency School plan been in force in the 'thirties, the Bank would have taken remedial action sooner and so (Pennington implied) "those alternations of excitement and depression" would have been less violent. This conversion to the strict Currency School view may have occurred before 1841;[3] certainly it can be dated before Pennington's surviving correspondence with Peel opens in 1844.

Pennington was, at the time of the correspondence, a well-established figure in the Political Economy Club, and, as we have seen, had been consulted first by the India Office and then by the Colonial Office and the Treasury. There is no indication as to how the 1844 correspondence opened, but it looks as though in April 1844 Pennington was helping Peel and Goulburn (Chancellor of the Exchequer) on the detailed figures of the settlement to be made between the Government and the Bank. The expected profits on the note-issue entered largely into this settlement, and Pennington had previously been useful for just this kind of calculation. Evidently following some previous paper, Pennington wrote advising Peel, 22nd April,[4] and enclosing a "Note on the profits of the promissory note circulation of the Bank of England," dated 20th April 1844. This takes as its basis the Currency School plan, as evolved in the discussions between Peel and Goulburn and

[1] B.M. Add. MSS. 40546, ff. 322–5. In his speech in the Commons debate on the Resolutions Wood had referred to Pennington's Paper, and had turned its argument to support of the Currency School plan now being put before Parliament by Peel (74 H.C. Deb. 3s. 20th May 1844, col. 1379).

[2] This must have been the Appendix, "Accounts relating to the Bank of England," in the Report and Mins. of Evid. of the Select Cttee on Banks of Issue (1840, iv). If I judge Pennington correctly, he must have enjoyed many days in poring over these 376 pages of figures covering the years 1832–40.

[3] On 4th February 1841 at the Political Economy Club Pennington supported Torrens in the latter's argument for a fixed fiduciary issue, but J. L. Prevost's diary note (P.E.C. *Centenary Volume*, p. 279) does not bear precise interpretation.

[4] BM. Add. MSS. 40543, ff. 49–58.

the representatives of the Bank,[1] and as eventually embodied in the Bank Charter Act. There is no comment on the scheme itself, Pennington's concern being exclusively with the financial settlement between the Government and the Bank. Peel wrote acknowledging receipt, and asking Pennington to call on him on the 27th at 11.45. There is no record of this interview, but subsequent references in their correspondence show that it did take place.

Before the interview on the 27th, Pennington had already written a "*Note on the scheme of a National Bank Proposed by the Author of 'Thoughts on the Currency'*."[2] He addressed this to Peel under date 25th April, so that it cannot be taken as arising out of the interview, but Peel did not actually receive it until afterwards. He then sent a polite but colourless acknowledgement.[3] The scheme propounded in this anonymous pamphlet[4] was for a note issue monopolized by a Government Commission, its amount to be fixed within wide limits, varying up and down within these limits according to whether the foreign exchanges were favourable or unfavourable. Pennington made two significant objections. He thought that it would so truncate the Bank of England that it would have to close, to the great inconvenience of the financial system. Secondly, he thought the provisions for varying the note issue too vague: "the only safe rule is to increase or diminish the paper according to the increase or diminution of the reserve of bullion, whatever that may be."

This *Note* justifies reference for two reasons only: in showing that Pennington by this date had become an uncompromising adherent of the Currency School, and for the light thrown on his character and his relationship with Peel. It was written before Pennington saw Peel and this, together with the bareness of Peel's acknowledgement, can be taken to mean that Pennington's advice on this pamphlet was not in response to particular request from Peel.

[1] Clapham, *The Bank of England* (Cambridge, 1944), Vol. 2, pp. 172–181.
[2] BM. Add. MSS. 40543 ff. 212–227.
[3] *Ibid.* Letter dated 27th April, 1844.
[4] Judging by the references Pennington makes to its contents, this must have been *Thoughts on the Currency*, published by Ridgway, London, 1842 (62 pp.) The author was familiar with the main publications in the controversy; I have not been able to identify him.

It is difficult to imagine that a man fully aware of the extent to which Peel was already set on the plan of the eventual Act would have believed that Peel would be interested in a detailed critique of a radically different proposal. It was not even as though the pamphlet's proposal represented the platform of the opposition school of thought, to which Peel would wish to refer in his principal speech in the forthcoming legislative process. The incident is consistent rather with the probability that Pennington was no party to the central discussions Peel and Goulburn had been holding with the Bank,[1] that he was called in as a technical expert to help get the figures right, and that, though flattered into the notion that Peel must be interested in his views on any relevant matter, he had no practical sense of the range of questions on which Peel remained open to persuasion.

This interpretation is consistent with the later correspondence between Pennington and Peel as well as other Ministers. In May 1844 he sent to Peel a memorandum commenting on a pamphlet just published by Sir William Clay;[2] these comments show Pennington as an uncompromising supporter of the Currency School plan, now being put before Parliament by Peel and Goulburn. A few weeks later, just before the Second Reading debates, Pennington sent to Peel a memorandum on the purchase and sale of bullion by the Bank of England.[3] Peel sent one acknowledgement—polite, but without any comment—covering both these Memoranda.[4]

During 1845 Pennington had further brief correspondence with Peel and Goulburn, on details arising in the Government's arrangements with the Bank of England,[5] and commenting—critically, of course—on Fullarton's

[1] For these discussions see Sir John Clapham, *The Bank of England* (Cambridge, 1944), Vol. 2, pp. 178–181.

[2] B.M. Add. MSS. 40544, ff. 24–28; the pamphlet was *Remarks on the Expediency of Restricting the Issue of Promissory Notes to a single Issuing Body* (London, 1844).

[3] BM. Add. MSS. 40545, f. 364. (The Memorandum is missing.)

[4] *Ibid.*, f. 364b.

[5] Letter, Peel to Pennington, 27th November 1845, BM. Add. MSS. 40579, ff. 394–5; Goulburn, letter from Pennington, 5th February 1845, and letter Goulburn to Pennington, 29th January 1845, both in Pennington Papers at the University of Chicago.

pamphlet, a second edition of which had just appeared.[1] Late in the year Peel was treating Pennington with marked confidence, for he referred to him reports sent by Cotton, who was not merely Governor of the Bank of England but one who stood out among his fellow Directors as a man to be peculiarly respected.[2] Cotton's reports were mainly concerned with the broader repercussions of the fantastic boom in railway companies, but he did refer particularly to the possibility of difficulties threatened in the banking world by certain large payments due to be made, under Parliamentary Standing Orders, in connection with subscriptions for railway shares. On this point Pennington seized, arguing that with careful handling by the Bank of England these large transfers of money could be smoothly effected, just as the West Indian Compensation loan (after emancipation of the slaves) had been handled. There is an uncharacteristic gusto about this memorandum, as though Pennington peculiarly enjoyed showing that he knew the Bank's business better even than the great Cotton himself; and he followed it up with a second memorandum. Peel, though he had taken the initiative in referring to Pennington, simply sent the whole batch of papers on to Goulburn; what the latter made of them does not emerge.[3]

In the spring of 1847, when the troubles culminating in the crisis of October 1847 were first showing themselves, Pennington volunteered further views. He addressed himself to Peel who, though now out of office and almost without a party, still in these matters commanded the attention of the House of Commons and of the Chancellor of the Exchequer. "I think it probable," wrote Pennington,[4]

[1] *On the Regulation of Currencies* (1st Edn. 1844, 2nd Edn. 1845). Pennington's letter to Peel, BM. Add. MSS. 40564, f. 81.

[2] When the 1844 legislation was in prospect, Ministers considered the possibility of instituting a permanent Governorship of the Bank. Peel then thought of Cotton as "the only fit man in the direction" for such office, and partly because Cotton, though he favoured the principle, refused to accept it for himself, the idea was dropped. (Letter, Peel to Goulburn, 27th August 1847, in the Goulburn Papers (Acc. 319, Box II/20) at the Surrey Record Office.)

[3] Letter, Peel to Goulburn, 3rd January 1846. This, with the other papers under reference, are in Acc. 319, Box II/20 at the Surrey Record Office.

[4] Letter (in an ageing hand), 12th April 1847, BM. Add. MSS. 40598, f. 160.

"that I shall wish to trouble you with a short memorandum on the commercial exchange with the United States of America." This memorandum does not seem to have materialized, but Pennington did at the same time send to Peel a copy of a memorandum he had addressed to the Chancellor of the Exchequer,[1] and in this he developed his view of how the 1844 legislation was working and should work. This was a long way from the intellectual toy the Currency Principle had become—to Pennington and others —during the 1830's; the view Pennington now took was a severely practical one, and the gilt was off the gingerbread. Summing up the proper effect of the Act, "the Bank is now *obliged*," he wrote, "to act with the prudence and forecast which were always necessary but not always practised"; but the Bank had nevertheless been too slack when gold was going out, and "It is now to be feared that the Bank will be obliged to 'pull up' suddenly, and with great inconvenience to the mercantile public, and to the Government."

In all this, there is nothing to indicate that Pennington played any major part in the process of ministerial consultation that evolved the Bank Charter Act of 1844 or in the discussions leading to the decision to leave the Act untouched after the crisis of 1847.[2] He was consulted on details, especially details of figures: the kind of consultation for which he had proved useful during the 'thirties. Securing thus a hearing, he volunteered views on the main issues, views that were consistent with the plans already formed by Ministers in their discussions with the Bank of England. There is no reason to question the account given by Clapham.[3] Pennington's important part was quite different; it was anterior to the ministerial consultations in which the plan was adopted. Pennington in 1827 originated the principle that the Bank should "keep the securities even," in his third Memorandum to Huskisson and, we may suppose, in discussions at the Political

[1] 9th April 1847, BM. Add. MSS. 40598, ff. 162–172.

[2] He was not a witness before either of the Parliamentary Committees that followed the crisis.

[3] *The Bank of England*, Vol. 2, pp. 178–181.

Economy Club.[1] Having been taken up by Horsley Palmer about 1829 or 1830, and aired in the 1832 Committee, the broad idea was developed during the 1830's when it was frequently the subject of discussion at the Political Economy Club and no doubt elsewhere. Palmer's attempt to mould the principle into a strategic approach to the daily problems of monetary control gave way, under the influence of doctrinaire temperaments, to the spurious simplicity of the Currency School's plan. Through S. J. Loyd and G. W. Norman (both members of the Club), the plan was taken up inside the Bank of England, and so reached—as recounted by Clapham—ministerial consideration. It had all begun with Pennington as a theoretical idea application of which would encounter, he thought, great practical difficulties. In the course of the 'thirties, the principle gained in popularity and the indications are that Pennington, as an energetic member of the Political Economy Club, played an important role in propagating the doctrine and, perhaps, in forgetting the difficulties he had originally seen in its way. When he looked back in 1847 the Bank Charter Act, as the framework of action, had already parted from its intellectual antecedents and had become—for Pennington as for others—a bludgeon to scare men of discretion into taking precautionary action sooner than they would otherwise have done. But Pennington was now an old man; he did not live into sterling's high summer, when the Bank Charter Act strangely became an object of veneration and men forgot the story that lay behind it, the story that Pennington had started.

Whether because he thought that the latest consultations had represented substantial service to the Government or—more probably—because his recent personal contact with Peel made direct application to the fount of rewards possible, Pennington in August 1844 wrote to Peel a long complaint of his treatment by Government departments, especially by the India Office.[2] After reciting the circumstances of his relations with departments (but

[1] Though not a member until 1828, Pennington was a visitor on some earlier occasions when currency was discussed (cf. above, p. xxii).

[2] BM. Add. MSS. 40549, ff. 388–390; 12th August, 1844

forgetting the £1500 compensation paid him by the India Office), he concluded: "it has thus happened that, during the greatest part of the time which has elapsed since I was induced in 1832 to abandon my commercial pursuits in order to devote my time and attention to the public service, I have been bound in shallows and perplexities. It is true indeed that I have had the consolation of thinking that the measures which I have suggested, as well at the India Board, as at the Treasury, have been attended with successful, and I believe, valuable results. But that reflection can hardly be regarded as alone a sufficient compensation for the expenditure of twelve of the best years of my life. Under this impression I have indulged the hope that I might be appointed to some station of a better and less doubtful character than that in which I am at present placed. That hope has hitherto been indulged in error."

Peel replied very politely. He wished it were in his power, he would have great confidence, etc. "But the civil Patronage at my disposal, such portion of it at least as is unconnected with Parliament or with professional employment has been so extremely limited and so inadequate when compared with the claims which have accumulated from my inability to meet them, that I have for some time past resolved to give no assurances however general in respect to the appointment to civil office—and thus avoid adding to the pain which I have felt in encouraging expectations which I have been unable to fulfil."[1]

In judging both this application and Peel's rejection of it, regard must be paid to the standards of the time, standards that were changing. When he first held senior ministerial office, Peel followed the custom of his time by providing handsomely—by public appointments—for his family and relations; these had priority.[2] As the years went by, others pressed their claims, and at the same time opportunities for lay appointments had become much scarcer and personal patronage of this kind was less taken for

[1] Letter, 17th August 1844, BM. Add. MSS. 40549, f. 391. Pennington very humbly accepted the position (40550, f. 190) and Peel wrote another polite note (f. 191).

[2] *Cf.* N. Gash, *Mr. Secretary Peel*, pp. 404–5.

granted.[1] By 1844, therefore, Peel was ready enough with a refusal which Pennington accepted as not open to persistent appeal such as had succeeded when he dragged the extra £1000 out of the India Office nine years earlier. There is no trace of any revival of the application in Peel's lifetime, and in the slight contacts he had with Ministers after Peel's death there is no sign that he tried with them. If Peel, who when Prime Minister had actually sent for Pennington, could not give Pennington "some station of a better and less doubtful character," there would be little point in applying to Ministers for whose legislative activities Pennington could claim no parentage. It seems probable that he continued to enjoy the £500 a year mentioned in his complaint to Peel, but he may have sighed enviously when Torrens was granted in 1852 a Civil List pension of £200.[2]

Meanwhile he continued now and then to provide odd pieces of expert advice for Ministers and their officials. There is some rather dull correspondence on the Bank Charter Act, with Trevelyan in 1855 and with Arbuthnot in 1861.[3] In 1852–53 he was consulted by the Treasury when minor questions arose on the relation between the Royal Mint's prices for gold, those at which the Bank of England operated, and the principal rates of foreign exchange;[4] Pennington had long been regarded as adept at just this kind of analysis. There are also, among the Gladstone Papers,[5] some papers on the decimal coinage question. In 1846 Pennington brushed the idea aside: "I have always regarded those schemes as the gambols and playfulness of idle ingenuity rather than as matters susceptible of any useful practical application." In 1854 he was asked to comment on the Report and Evidence taken by

[1] N. Gash, *Politics in the Age of Peel* (London, 1953), pp. 349–352.
[2] U.K. *Accounts and Papers*, 1852, XXVIII, Finance (563) 260. Torrens had, on 12th July 1844, written to Peel asking for office, and received a curt refusal (BM. Add. MSS. 40548, ff. 211–213 and 215–216). I owe all these references relating to Torrens to Professor F. W. Fetter.
[3] Both these were Treasury officials. The letters are in the James Pennington Papers at the University of Chicago.
[4] *Welby Collection* (London School of Economics, Col. R.I.), ff. 30–38, 42–45 and 136–142.
[5] BM. Add. MSS. 44580, ff. 22–23.

the recent Committee of enquiry;[1] the burden of his reply was that the Committee had underestimated the difficulties of transition, and that these difficulties and "the inconvenience and injury . . . to the working classes . . . would not be counterbalanced by the real or supposed advantages which Banks, merchants, &c. would derive from it." I find the assurance of this attitude a little surprising: in 1827 Pennington had been more ready to put forward a theoretical adventure.

Although there were these occasional references in the last ten years of Pennington's life, there is no sign that any great weight was attached to his views. The Political Economy Club, which had once been his most effective contact with the world of policy-makers, inevitably saw little of Pennington in his declining years.[2] Peel was the last Minister to take an initiative in consulting him, and it may be that after Peel's death the Treasury simply referred occasional questions to him in order to justify continuance of the annual payment of £500. Pennington was quick to seize these opportunities for exercising his analytical powers and his knowledge of monetary history, and the memoranda would duly emerge, with deferential notes in increasingly shaky handwriting, from the house on Clapham Common. The financial "shallows and perplexities" of which Pennington had complained to Peel in 1844 apparently remained with him to the end, for when he died on 23rd March 1862 he left "less than £3000," a fortune small indeed for a "retired merchant" of the City of London.[3] He had named as an executor his son Edward, described as a Senior Clerk in the War Office.[4] Perhaps the son's nomination to this Department was a bone thrown out by Ministers to the humble expert who rather liked having his brains picked by men of high estate.

[1] Select Committee on Decimal Coinage, 1852–53.

[2] Until 1846 he had attended most meetings, but he went only twice after 1852 (P.E. Club *Minutes*, Vol. IV).

[3] He so described himself in the 1851 Census Return.

[4] The will is dated 9th March 1855. (Principal Probate Registry (ref. 405/1862), Somerset House, London.)

OBSERVATIONS ON THE PRIVATE BANKING ESTABLISHMENTS OF THE METROPOLIS

(First Memorandum to Huskisson, 1826)

Acknowledgements of debt which are convertible into the Coin of the realm at the pleasure of those to whom they are due, and which, on the faith of that convertibility, are employed as the medium of exchange, are of two kinds; namely, the promissory Notes of Bankers payable on demand, and the transferable book debts of bankers likewise payable on demand. Of these the latter are the principal medium of interchange in the commercial transactions of the metropolis.

The seventy private banking Establishments of the metropolis are commonly regarded merely as banks of deposit: they are however essentially circulating banks, differing from the country banks which circulate their promissory notes payable on demand, only in the mode in which their business is transacted. The money placed in their hands consists, in the first instance, solely of bank of England notes and Coin, and it is evident that if the whole were retained by them, no advantage whatever would be derived from the deposits. They are permitted, therefore, to make what use they please of the money entrusted to their care, on the sole condition of being able to discharge with promptitude and regularity the fluctuating and occasional demands made upon them by the depositors. If a reserve of one half were sufficient for this purpose, the other half would be employed in discounting bills of Exchange, in the purchase of Exchequer bills, in advances upon Stock, or in any other way that might be deemed prudent and desirable. But the Persons to whom these advances, or from whom these purchases were made, would, for their own convenience, deposit the money to which they had become entitled, in the hands of their respective bankers, and the aggregate amount of the outstanding balances due from *all* the bankers, would, from that moment, be encreased 50 per cent. and against them they would be in possession of two thirds of their amount in bank of England notes and coin, and of one third in Commercial Bills discounted, Exchequer Bills purchased &c. The money due to all the depositors would be 50 per cent. more than it was previously to the commencement of these operations, and many of them would find that they had more money at their bankers than was sufficient for their current and ordinary purposes. This excess of money would not fail to produce the usual consequences of Excess, namely, an augmentation of prices, a depression of the foreign exchange, and a contraction of the issues of the bank of England, until at length the exportation of gold, and the abstraction of bank notes, would reduce the aggregate amount of the balances due to the various depositors, to the amount at which it stood previously to any investments having been made by the bankers.

If we suppose that when the operations above described began, the persons to whom the advances upon commercial bills &c., were made, declined placing the money they had acquired, in the hands of a banker, and passed it into circulation through other channels,—still, as the balances due to the former depositors would not thereby be lessened, the whole quantity of money, or of what performs the functions of money, would be encreased to the extent above mentioned, and the usual consequences of excess would inevitably ensue.

It thus appears that it is in the power of the London bankers to augment the balances they owe to their various customers by operations that originate with themselves, and it is obvious that the aggregate amount of these balances cannot be reduced without a corresponding reduction of their bank notes and gold, or of the productive securities in their possession, or of both. But these balances are money, perform all the functions of money, act upon the prices of commodities in the same manner as bank notes and coin, and are equally efficient in their purchasing power. They are transferable book debts convertible into bank notes and coin at the pleasure of those to whom they are due. The promissory notes of country bankers are essentially the same thing; they are a different form of the same species of credit.

It will simplify the consideration of this subject if we suppose that instead of seventy private banking establishments in London there are only two, and that these two are of sufficient consequence and credit to engross all the business of the metropolis. These two banking Establishments will, then, be the depositories of all the money which the merchants, traders &c. of London deem it necessary to keep in readiness to answer their current and occasional demands, and as the bankers are at liberty to make use of any part of it they please for their own benefit, they will hold against the balances due to their various customers, a comparatively small amount of bank of England notes and coin, and a large amount of commercial bills, exchequer bills, and other productive securities, the interest arising from which constitutes their profit. The aggregate amount of these funds will be equal to the aggregate amount of the balances due to the various depositors, and the whole or any part of the balances transferred from one account to another will perform exactly the same functions as a like amount of promissory notes would do, circulating amongst the depositors.

It will perhaps be said that the aggregate amount of the deposits will depend solely upon the pleasure and convenience of the depositors, and cannot, like the promissory notes circulating in the Country, be increased or diminished at the pleasure of the banker. What is to prevent it? Suppose the deposits in each bank to be ten millions, and that, against these, each has in productive securities eight millions, in bank notes and coin two millions; under these circumstances, one of them, encouraged by the flattering state of public and commercial credit, is induced to advance an additional million upon commercial or government securities, and to this end directs cheques to be drawn upon him in favour of the persons to whom the advances are made. The probability is that one half of the cheques so drawn, will be paid into his own bank, and increase the amount of its outstanding balances to the extent of £500,000; the other half will be paid into the neighbouring bank, and increase *its* balances to the same extent. The cash reserve of the first bank will then be one and a half millions, the cash reserve of the second bank, two and a half millions. The bank whose cash is increased will now be disposed to extend its productive investment, and will, in like manner direct cheques to be drawn upon it for the purchase of commercial or government securities to the extent of one million. Of these cheques one half will be paid into that bank, the other half into the neighbouring bank. The outstanding balances of each will now be eleven millions, the cash reserve of each two millions, and the productive securities in the possession of each, nine millions. What in London performs all the purposes of money will be increased two millions. The superstructure will be enlarged altho' the basis remains the same.

In the imaginary case here stated it is supposed that the operations of the two bankers, which produce an extension of the currency, take place suddenly and at once. In reality, however, it is likely they would be slow and gradual. Each banker would be disposed to extend his discounts and increase his purchases by little and little, and a considerable time would probably elapse before they attained the extent above stated.

It may perhaps be thought that such a process as is here described might possibly take place if there were only two banking establishments; but that where there are so many as seventy, they will be a check upon each other, and that if any one of them should venture to extend its credit circulation beyond the usual bounds, it would be warned of its error by an inconvenient diminution of its cash reserve: all the cheques drawn upon this bank for the amount of its new investments may be paid into the hands of other bankers, and a regard to its own security would then be an inducement to re-discount or re-sell them.

This would be true if the advances were hastily and injudiciously made, and it is precisely this consideration which restrains country bankers, whose circulation is within the same sphere, or in the same neighbourhood, from too sudden and injudicious an extension of their issues. There are in Edinburgh five or six circulating banks, of which the notes of each are continually falling into the hands of the others. Twice a week they exchange notes with each other, and liquidate the balances arising therefrom, by a payment of bank of England notes, or by a short dated bill upon London, exactly upon the same principle, and with the same intention that require the daily liquidation, at the clearing house, of the cheques upon each other, by the London bankers. If any one of the Edinburgh banks were unduly to increase its issues, a greater number than usual of its notes would fall into the hands of the neighbouring banks, and that bank would have a larger balance than usual to pay, in bank of England notes, at the periods of weekly liquidation. Each is thus a restraint upon the other, and they are all obliged to manage their business with care and circumspection. But neither the extension of the book credits of the London, nor an increased circulation of country, notes, takes place so suddenly, nor to so great an extent, as to create the inconvenience here alluded to. It is slowly and gradually, when credit is high and expectation on the wing, and in times of extraordinary excitement, that bankers are induced greatly to extend their circulation,—each feeling confident that at such a period, his competitors will pursue the same course, and, by so doing, prevent the inconvenient payment to each other of large balances at the periods of mutual liquidation. Upon such occasions the circulation generally becomes excessive, and is not unfrequently carried to a dangerous bearing.

On the other hand, during a period of distrust and difficulty the reverse of these operations takes place. Each banker is desirous to increase his cash reserve, and to lessen the amount of his outstanding engagements. But if the amount of bank notes and gold in the hands of the seventy London bankers, collectively, remain the same, the aggregate amount of their outstanding engagements can be lessened only by parting with a portion of their productive securities. To part with any portion of their productive securities will, necessarily, diminish their balances. There will be less of what is called money; and the pressure and the difficulty occasioned by such a contraction of the currency will, in all probability, continue, until falling prices, a rise of the foreign exchange, and an influx of bullion, have restored the currency to its proper level.

In ordinary times, when there prevails no extraordinary excitement, nor any remarkable depression, the deposits in the hands of the seventy London bankers may be estimated, roundly, at 35 millions, the bank of England notes and gold at 7 millions, and the productive securities at 28 millions. Thirty five millions are erected upon the basis of seven millions. Seven millions are made to perform all the functions which, if the London banking system had no existence, would require thirty five millions; and the question is whether the balances amounting to thirty five millions may be increased or diminished without any increase or diminution of the basis on which they rest.

The process by which they may be increased has already been described. The process by which they may be diminished is not less obvious, and, by the peculiar circumstances of the present time is rendered strikingly manifest. The London bankers have been exposed to the influence of an extraordinary panic. The powerful as well as the weak have endeavoured to protect themselves by increasing their reserve of bank notes. But of bank notes the quantity in London is limited, and that portion of them which circulates amongst those who do not require the intervention of a banker, cannot, if we suppose their ordinary payments to be made with the usual regularity admit of any material diminution. A London banker, therefore, can increase his stock of bank notes only by withdrawing them from some one or all of the other bankers. He may go into the market and sell stock and exchequer bills, or re-discount the commercial bills on which he has already made advances. If he do this, he will receive a cheque upon his own or some other bank. A cheque upon his own bank will diminish his outstanding balances, without increasing his stock of bank notes. A cheque upon some other banker will increase his stock of bank notes at the expence of that other banker, and pro tanto diminish the bank notes as well as the outstanding balances of that other banker; who, in his turn, at such a period of alarm, will be desirous to get back his bank notes, and, to that end, will bring stock, exchequer bills, &c. to market, and possibly sell them to those who have deposits in the hands of that very banker who had previously succeeded in withdrawing them from him. Fear and distrust thus acting and re-acting will inevitably diminish the amount of the balances due from all the bankers collectively. The amount of bank notes in the hands of each may fluctuate considerably, but the amount in the hands of all can vary but little. There will be a contest with each other for bank notes; themselves and their customers injuring each other in the struggle.

But a diminution of the balances in the hands of all the bankers is a diminution of the money of the metropolis. At the present moment it is probable that altho' the amount of bank of England notes in the hands of all the London bankers is greater than usual, the aggregate amount of their outstanding balances is considerably less. It is obvious indeed that if all of them were to allow the commercial bills in their hands to become due, without in the meantime discounting any other bills, not only would the merchants, but many of the bankers themselves be reduced to extreme difficulty. The thirty five millions of balances might in no long time be reduced to twenty millions, or perhaps to fifteen millions. At present, owing to the distrust which greatly prevails, they are, it is probable, considerably reduced, and until confidence be restored will continue comparatively low.

In 1793 the amount of bank of England notes in circulation was not materially less than usual, but the want of money in the Metropolis was extreme. Transferable book credits, of which the money of London in a great measure consists, were refused to commercial bills, and it was not until confidence was restored by a loan of Exchequer bills, that they were readily granted.

Clapham 13 Feb[y] 1826
Js Pennington.

LETTER ADDRESSED TO THE AUTHOR BY JAMES PENNINGTON, ESQ.

(being Appendix C of Volume 2 of *Tooke's History of Prices*)

DEAR SIR,

It was the principal object of the paper of observations, which you did me the honour to append to your published letter to Lord Grenville, to illustrate the principle on which the deposits of the London bankers are formed, and the mode in which they act; to show that they are susceptible of considerable increase, or diminution, without a corresponding enlargement or contraction of the basis on which they rest; and that, consequently, the quantity of money in the metropolis may be greater, or less, at one time than another, although the circulation of the Bank of England should remain uniformly the same.

I did not attempt, in that paper, to explain all the various circumstances which tend to augment, or to lessen, the amount of the deposits. My object was to show that the book credits of a London banker, and the promissory notes of a country banker, are essentially the same thing; that they are different forms of the same kind of credit; and that they are employed to perform the same functions.

It never occurred to me, as appears to have been supposed by Colonel Torrens, that every million of notes issued by the Bank of England forms the basis of five millions of deposits; and that every million withdrawn from circulation, by the Bank, occasions a five-fold diminution of those deposits. On the contrary, it is perfectly consistent with my view of the subject, to suppose that the deposit accounts of the London bankers may be materially diminished, while the circulation of the Bank of England is greatly enlarged, or *vice versa*.

Colonel Torrens, in his published letter to Lord Melbourne, appears to have fallen into some misapprehension on this head.

He thinks that if, between December, 1833, and March, 1834, the Bank of England had contracted its circulation to the extent of 1,447,000*l.*, that contraction would have occasioned a diminution of the book-credit circulation of the metropolis of five times that amount.

In this statement he appears to have overlooked the circumstance, that, of the outstanding notes of the Bank of England, by far the largest portion is not in the hands of the London bankers, but in the hands of those the nature and routine of whose business do not require the employment of a banker; and that when a million of notes are cancelled by bullion payments, it is probable that the greatest part of that amount is finally withdrawn, not from the hands of the bankers, but from the external circulation.

It has been objected to the views which I endeavoured to explain, that as the amount of deposits left in the hands of a banker depends upon the pleasure and convenience of the depositors, the banker has no power to increase the quantity of money in circulation, without increasing or diminishing the fund which he reserves to meet the occasional demands of the depositors.

This is true: and it is equally true that, as the amount of notes which a bank of circulation is able to keep out depends upon the convenience and the willingness of those into whose hands they fall to hold them, the quantity of outstanding paper money is necessarily limited by that circumstance.

But the question is, whether the pleasure and the convenience of the depositors, and the will and the disposition of the note holders, are susceptible, at different times, of any material alteration in this respect; and, if they are, whether the deposit banks, and the circulating banks, can turn that alteration to their own advantage without entrenching on their reserved fund.

In order to determine this question, it is necessary to examine the circumstances that limit the amount of deposits, and of outstanding notes.

It has been correctly stated, by more than one writer on this subject, that the quantity of money in circulation is limited by the necessity which every one feels, or the endeavour which every one uses, to keep at his banker's, in his till, or in his pocket, no greater sum than he deems to be sufficient to answer current and occasional demands. One person keeps 5000*l.* for this purpose; another 500*l.*, another 100*l.*; and so on, to a few sovereigns, or a few shillings.

The aggregate amount of the money so kept forms the sum total of the money in circulation.

Now, if all the circulating banks simultaneously issue a greater amount of notes than can be absorbed in this way, some person, or many persons, must have in their possession a greater sum of money than is sufficient for current purposes.

Of this excess the ultimate corrective is the foreign exchange. A considerable time may, however, elapse before the check begins to operate. The foreign exchange is affected only through the medium of prices, or of the rate of interest; but an unusual abundance of money does not always produce a general rise of prices. It is quite possible, indeed, that contemporaneously with that abundance, the prices of commodities may be generally low. The increased issue of paper may fall into the hands of those who, from habit and inclination, are averse from investing their money savings in commodities, or services, with a view to reproduction and to profit; but whose desire it is to employ the money which comes into their hands, over and above their own personal and unproductive expenditure, in such a way as will bring to them an increased income, with as little risk and trouble as possible. But the opportunity of so employing this surplus money may not immediately occur. The amount of the public funds, in time of peace, is generally stationary or diminishing. If, therefore, one person determine, however high may be the price, to invest his money savings in the public funds, another person must necessarily be forced out; and the money, in the shape of Bank notes, or of book credits, may still remain waiting for an investment.

In such a state of things, there frequently prevails great dulness of demand for commodities, and a low rate of interest.

In the long run, however, it is probable that, either in consequence of an actual or prospective rise of prices, or in consequence of the demand of the saving class of the community for foreign stocks and foreign investments, the foreign exchange will become depressed, and a demand for metallic money for exportation be created; which demand, the bankers will be obliged, directly or indirectly, to satisfy. A contraction of the currency will then in all probability take place, and the redundant money disappear.

It thus appears that the promissory notes of the provincial bankers, and the book credits of the London bankers, may be issued to a greater extent than is necessary for the purpose of internal interchange; that the surplus of money, so created, may remain inert for a considerable time, without raising the prices of commodities, or affecting the foreign exchange; and that the ultimate corrective of the excess is a demand for, and exportation of, metallic money.

It may perhaps be said, that although circulating banks may occasionally issue an excessive quantity of paper, in the manner above described, it is impossible that the London banks, which are merely banks of deposit, can err in this respect. *They* can only lend to others the money which has been previously lent to them. *They* do not create paper money; they only employ, in discounting bills of exchange, or in advances upon securities bearing interest, the metallic or the paper money which has been placed in their hands for the purpose of facilitating the money transactions of the depositors. *They* are merely cashiers.

But although the London bankers do not issue promissory notes, it is quite certain that they do not create "promises to pay," which perform the functions, and serve all the purposes of promissory notes, and which may be increased without intrenching on their reserved fund, or diminished without adding to it?

What takes place when a London banker, or a country banker, discounts a bill of exchange?

When a London banker discounts a bill of exchange, he gives credit for the amount of the bill, less the interest, for the period which the bill has to run, in an account opened in his ledger: when a country banker discounts a bill of exchange, he pays the amount of the bill, less the interest, in promissory notes. In both cases payment from the banker of the amount of the bill, less the discount, may be immediately demanded in gold, or in Bank of England notes.

It may be said, that unless the person in whose favour the advance is made allows the money to remain in deposit, the London banker will immediately be called upon for payment; while the notes of the country banker may remain, for a considerable time, outstanding.

But does it necessarily follow, that if a cheque be drawn upon the London banker for the amount of the advance, he will be obliged to intrench upon his reserved fund? The cheque may be paid into his hands by some other depositor, and placed at the credit of that other depositor; in which case, other things remaining the same, the whole amount of the book credits of that banker will be increased to the extent of this new advance. And even if the cheque be paid into the hands of some other banker, the amount of the book credits of the banker who has paid the cheque will not be diminished, while the book credits, as well as the reserved fund of the banker, to whom it is paid, will be increased by its amount.

Now, precisely the same train of circumstances may happen with regard to the notes of a country banker. In the first instance he issues fresh notes for the amount of the bill discounted. So long as these additional notes remain in circulation, he is precisely in the situation of a London banker to whom a cheque upon himself has been paid by a depositor.

But the additional notes may fall into the hands of a neighbouring bank; in which case the banker who issued them will be called upon for their discharge; and the reserved fund of the banker into whose hands they had fallen will be increased by the amount of the notes.

In consequence of this accession to his reserved fund, the second banker will be enabled to enlarge his issues; and thus the quantity of circulating paper may be augmented.

The converse of these operations may take place. The

new advances, instead of being again deposited or circulated in the form of notes, may be employed in the discharge of securities previously in the possession of the bank; in which case there will be no augmentation of money.

Moreover, some of the deposits or notes already outstanding may be employed in the same way; in which case there will be a diminution of the quantity of money, unless the cancelled notes or cancelled deposits be reinstated by fresh discounts and fresh advances.

It does not appear to me that this reasoning is affected by an observation which I have sometimes heard, that circulating banks have frequently the power to force out and extend their issues of notes, while the London bankers are generally passive in this respect, and allow their book credit circulation to be increased, or diminished, by some extrinsic force which they themselves have not been directly instrumental in producing.

That there may occasionally be some difference in the practical working of the two kinds of machinery I may readily admit, and yet still maintain that the character and object of both are essentially the same; that both the one and the other are substitutes for a metallic currency, and are susceptible of considerable increase or diminution, without a corresponding enlargement or contraction of the basis on which they rest.

But is it true, in point of fact, that the one has constantly and uniformly an advantage over the other in this respect? Has it not sometimes happened that, while the country bankers have found it impossible to increase their issues of notes, but on the contrary have been obliged to curtail them, the London bankers have been able to continue their usual operations, and even to extend them?

You, who are accurately acquainted with all the material facts and circumstances of our past commercial history, can answer these questions. I apprehend the truth to be, that each mode of circulation is affected by a variety of circumstances which do not always simultaneously affect both.

Permit me, in this place, to notice some observations that have been published on this subject.

With the view of explaining the principle and the operations of a bank of deposit, it has been said that the deposits left by individuals in the hands of a banker are *monied capital*, of which the functions are performed by a comparatively small sum of money; and that the banker is compensated for his trouble by employing, for his own benefit, that portion of the deposits which is not used by the depositor.

Of the meaning of the expression *monied capital*, no explanation is given. If metallic money is not intended by it, the expression can mean only land, houses, merchandise, and other things of a like nature, in which what is called monied capital consists; for surely it cannot mean the parchment, or the paper, on which the right to, or the interest in, the property referred to, is recorded. The banker may not be able to point out a single tangible and visible object on which any part of the written securities in his possession finally depends. Still, those securities (if they are good securities), whether consisting of bills, bonds, mortgage deeds, or pledges of stock, have reference to property in which the deposits left in the hands of a banker are actually invested.

If this is a correct view of the matter, the expression, "monied capital," in the observations referred to, means certain muniments of title which are readily convertible, by sale or otherwise, into metallic money at the pleasure of the holder.

The result then is, that the deposits in the hands of a banker consist of debts of that banker to the depositors, against which debts he holds a small sum of money and other debts and obligations, which are finally resolvable into some tangible and visible object, its usufruct, or its produce.

In this sense of the term "monied capital," it may be admitted that the deposits in the hands of a banker are monied capital.

In a like sense it must be admitted that the promissory notes of a circulating bank are monied capital, which monied capital, if traced out to the things in which it is really invested or embodied, will be found to consist of houses, land, merchandise, &c., into which certain debts in the form of bankers' promissory notes are finally resolvable.

What is meant when it is said that the *functions* of this capital are performed by a small sum of money, is not quite so obvious.

The facts of the case are, however, sufficiently obvious.

A banker knows, from experience, that, although most of the debts which he owes are payable on demand, payment of a comparatively small portion of them is likely to be suddenly demanded. Of the funds entrusted to him he reserves, therefore, in the form of cash, no greater sum than he deems to be sufficient to answer that small amount of demand. This reserved cash performs no other function than the occasional payment of some of the debts owing by the banker.

I must here again beg to observe, that although the transferable book debts and the promissory notes of bankers are employed as a substitute for metallic money, it does not follow that every increase or diminution of their amount will necessarily affect prices of commodities in a degree commensurate with that increase or diminution. It may, and often does, happen that a larger portion than usual of the actual amount has fallen into the hands, or is at the disposal of, persons who are unwilling for a season to bring their money funds to market. When this is the case, then —given the quantity of book credit money, and of notes— if those who are indisposed to come to market with their money have a larger share than usual, others must have a less share than usual.

This state of things may occur in a country of which the currency is exclusively metallic. When it does occur, prices are generally low, and the exchanges favourable to an influx of the metals.

It may, moreover, be observed, that the substitution of transferable book debts for metallic money induces, by the facility of transfer, and the safe custody which it affords, many persons to keep at their disposal much larger balances of money than they would be disposed to keep if the currency were wholly metallic. These extra balances render the quantity of money, or what answers all the purposes of money, much greater in this country than it probably would be if the currency consisted exclusively of coin. They are not to be regarded as so much unemployed capital. The capital which they represent exists in a tangible form somewhere; they are credits available at a moment's notice by the parties in whose favour they are given. They do not act upon the prices of commodities, or of securities, unless they are brought out. They are merely so much dormant credit. The large sums lodged, at interest, in the Scotch, and in many of the provincial banks, are of this description, with this difference, that they are not payable on demand without previous notice to the banker.

It remains to consider the deposits of the Bank of England, and to enquire in what respect they differ from its note circulation. It may be proper to consider them under the following heads:—

1. Deposits of Government.
2. Deposits of the London bankers.
3. Drawing accounts.

The most important question that occurs with regard to these deposits is this:— Upon which of them, and in what degree, is a demand for gold, when it arises either from the internal wants of the country, or from an unfavourable balance of trade, likely to fall; and what effect is that demand likely to have upon the note circulation of the Bank?

Let us take them in their order.

1. The Government balances.

Of these the aggregate amount varies; first, in consequence of the greater or less productiveness of the public revenue compared with the expenditure; and secondly, because, when the income and expenditure are, on the whole, even, the former is not, for short periods of time, commensurate with the outgoings. From these causes, and in consequence of the necessity of a strict adherence to the rules of parliamentary appropriation, the Government balances are subject to temporary fluctuations. But as the variations, in the course of the year, usually compensate each other, their effect on prices, or on the rate of interest, and, through prices or the rate of interest, on the foreign exchange, is too inconsiderable to deserve notice.

When the revenue is surplus, the excess is brought into circulation through the medium of the sinking-fund, or is applied to the redemption of quarterly deficiency bills, agreeably to the provisions of the Act of 10 Geo. IV., cap. 27.

When the revenue is deficient, the deficiency must be made good in some other way than by a direct advance from the Bank of England, or the general circulation will, no doubt, be artificially enlarged.

2. Deposits of the London bankers.

These constitute part of the reserved fund of the London bankers, which it may be presumed is kept in deposit at the Bank solely to suit the convenience of the bankers, the custody of the Bank being preferred to that of their own iron chests.

The increase or diminution of these balances depends upon the general state of the money circulation of the metropolis. If, during the prevalence of an unfavourable foreign exchange, the balances are reduced by cheques drawn upon the Bank, and finally by payments in gold, for exportation, then—unless the bankers themselves export the gold on their own account, which seldom or never happens—the balances due to their various depositors, and consequently the quantity of money in the metropolis, is as effectually reduced as if the outstanding notes of the Bank were reduced by the redemption of securities in its possession, and the bankers' deposits at the Bank to remain unaltered.

On the other hand, during the prevalence of a favourable foreign exchange, and the consequent influx of gold from abroad, whether the imported gold is held by the bankers, or placed by them in deposit at the Bank, the quantity of money in the metropolis is as effectually increased as it would be if the Bank of England were to give notes in exchange for the gold.

3. Drawing accounts.

These are to be regarded exactly in the same light as so many drawing accounts kept with private bankers; they are transferable book-debts in a constant state of active circulation.

The propriety and expediency of separating the deposit department from the circulating department of the Bank, have lately been suggested in the belief that such a separation would render the operations of the Bank more conformable to certain rules, the strict observance of which, it is supposed, can alone make the currency vary exactly as it would do if it were wholly and exclusively metallic.

It is proposed that the circulating department shall hold a fixed amount of securities, and that its issue of notes beyond that amount shall be confined to the exchange of gold for notes, and notes for gold, with a few exceptions of no essential or material importance.

It is further proposed that the deposit department shall be free to employ its funds in whatever manner is most conducive to profit, and at the same time consistent with prudence and good management.

Although there is at present, I apprehend, no confusion of accounts between the two departments, yet so complete a separation of them as that which has been suggested, could not well be effected without a more formal division of debts and assets than mere book-keeping can accomplish. Whether a deposit bank upon so large a scale as that of the Bank of England could be so conducted as to prevent considerable fluctuations in the value of the currency, I own I have considerable doubts.

I am, dear Sir,

Very faithfully yours,

JAMES PENNINGTON.

Clapham, April 10. 1838.

A LETTER

TO

KIRKMAN FINLAY, ESQ.,

ON THE

IMPORTATION

OF

FOREIGN CORN,

AND

THE VALUE OF THE PRECIOUS METALS IN DIFFERENT COUNTRIES.

TO WHICH ARE ADDED

OBSERVATIONS ON MONEY, AND THE FOREIGN EXCHANGE.

By JAMES PENNINGTON, Esq.

LONDON:
SIMPKIN, MARSHALL, & CO., AND PELHAM RICHARDSON;
CLAPHAM, D. BATTEN.

1840.

ADVERTISEMENT.

The Letter on the Importation of Foreign Corn, and the Value of the Precious Metals in different countries, was written in the early part of last year.

In the Observations on Currency and Coinage, much of what relates to coinage was submitted to the late Mr. Huskisson, in the year 1827. The memorandum on the management of the Bank of England was drawn up at his request.

Clapham Common, June, 1840.

LETTER

ON THE

IMPORTATION OF FOREIGN CORN.

MY DEAR SIR,

I believe we agree in the opinion, that in the present excited state of the public mind on the subject of the Corn Laws, great exaggeration is manifested on both sides of the question—that the advocates for the total repeal of those laws, and the unrestrained admission of foreign corn, are looking forward to great and extraordinary advantages which it is not likely will ever be realized—and, that their opponents are fearful that a free trade in corn would be attended with a degree of loss and disaster to all classes of the community, of which there is no reasonable ground for the apprehension.

A calm and dispassionate enquiry into a subject of this kind is not, perhaps, to be expected. I will endeavour, however, with all the care and impartiality of which I am capable, to examine the statements and the apprehensions of the contending parties, and state my own sentiments and views with regard to the important question at issue.

I propose, in the first instance, to treat the question abstractedly; for, although it may be said that the abstract case is not the practical one, yet I apprehend it will, at the same time, be allowed, that in this way only can a just analysis be formed, and that, when that is accomplished, we shall be able the better to judge of the complex case as it exists in reality.

The points which it is most material to examine are, first, the effect which the free admission of foreign corn into the ports of this country would have upon the price of corn, and upon the condition of our domestic agriculture; and secondly, the ultimate incidence of duties levied on its importation.

When the question is asked, What is the precise nature and extent of the advantage which, it may reasonably be expected, will result from the free admission of foreign corn? the common and usual answer is, "greater cheapness." But when this answer is given to the question, it becomes necessary to enquire what is meant by the term "cheapness," in this particular application of it. Does the expression mean merely a fall in the money price? But a fall in the money price of corn may result from an enhancement in the value of money—from the greater difficulty, for instance, with which the metal of which money is made is obtained at the mines, occasioning a fall, not in the money price of corn only, but of corn in common with all other commodities. Such a fall of general prices would, undoubtedly, be advantageous to those who enjoy fixed money incomes, and proportionately disadvantageous to those from whose capital and industry the fixed money incomes are ultimately derived. This, surely, is not the result contemplated by the advocates for a free trade in corn. By the term "cheapness" I apprehend they mean a fall in the price of corn relatively to that of all other commodities—all other things retaining the same value relatively to each other, and to money, as before, corn falling relatively to them all. In short, they mean, not merely a fall in the *price* of corn, but likewise a fall in its *relative value.* The importance of the distinction will be seen hereafter.

Those who contend for a free trade in corn say, that in ordinary years a supply of wheat may be obtained from abroad at about 40*s.* per quarter, and other grain in proportion; that the requisite supply of home grown wheat cannot be obtained at less than 60*s.* per quarter; and that, by the exclusion of foreign corn from the home market, or the exaction of a high duty on its importation, a pecuniary burden of enormous amount is entailed on the consumers of agricultural produce in this country.

In thus stating their case, they appear to assume, that if the importation of foreign corn were permitted, duty free, the price of home grown corn would fall to the price at which foreign corn can be imported, and to infer from that assumption, that a free trade in corn would benefit the consumers of corn in this country to the extent of the difference between the two prices.

As this party appear to rest their arguments mainly on this ground, it is necessary carefully to examine it, and if it be found untenable, then to enquire at what point the prices of foreign corn, and home corn brought to the same market, would ultimately coincide.

Before going into that examination and enquiry, it will be useful succinctly to state the principles which regulate the rise and fall of *rent.*

The rent of land has been defined to be "that portion of the value of the whole produce which remains to the owner, after all the outgoings, of whatever kind, belonging to its cultivation, have been paid, including the profits of the capital employed, estimated according to the usual and ordinary rate of the profits of agricultural stock at the time being."

It follows, from this definition, that when the produce of the land is only just sufficient to restore those outgoings, and to yield that profit, there can be no rent, and that all the land which yields a greater return than this, is capable of paying rent equal to the value of the excess.

Suppose that the land of the greatest natural fertility in actual cultivation yields twenty-four bushels per acre, that the next best land yields twenty-three bushels, and so on, down to twelve bushels per acre, then the *corn* rent of the best land will be twelve bushels, of the next best land eleven bushels, and so on, down to one bushel per acre. The *money* rent will depend on the natural price of corn, and the natural price of corn will depend on the money outgoings necessary to produce the corn on that land which yields no rent, together with the usual and ordinary rate of profit on the capital employed.

If 60*s*. per quarter be the price which is just sufficient for that end, the money rent of the land which produces twenty-four bushels per acre will be 4*l*. 10*s*. per acre, and the money rent of the land which produces only thirteen bushels will be 7*s*. 6*d*. per acre; and if a farm which contains thirteen hundred acres of land, of all the various qualities of soil, from the best to the worst, but none so little fertile as not to yield twelve bushels per acre, the rent of that farm, spread over the whole number of acres, supposing the whole to be cultivated, will be 2*l*. 5*s*. 7*d*. per acre.

But, although this will be the real rent, it will not always be the actual or conventional rent.

The real rent must vary according to the accidental variations of the produce; but as the landlord is always anxious not to get less, and the tenant is averse from ever paying more than the real rent, the real and the conventional rent must, in the long run, nearly coincide.

Before the nature and source of rent were fully explained and understood, a mistake was frequently made "in applying, to the employment of capital in obtaining raw produce, the same maxims which regulate the employment of capital in manufacturing raw produce, or, to use a more convenient but less accurate expression, in considering agriculture and manufactures as governed by the same rules. They are, in fact, the subject of one fundamental distinction. The distinction may be thus stated: every additional capital employed in manufactures produces the same, or a greater proportionate net return, while every additional capital employed in agriculture produces a smaller proportionate net return; or, conversely, every diminution of capital employed in manufactures occasions no alteration in the proportionate net return, while every diminution of capital employed in agriculture is followed by a larger proportinate net return."

The most approved writers on political economy agree, I think, in this account of the nature and source of rent, and of the difference between manufactures and agricultural produce, although they differ with respect to some minor considerations which do not affect the general principle.

We may now return to the representations of those who call for the free admission of foreign corn, and to the assumption on which those representations are founded.

It is said that the price of corn grown in England being 60*s*., and the price of foreign corn 40*s*. per quarter, if the free admission of foreign corn were permitted, the price of home grown corn would fall to the price at which foreign corn can be imported, that is, from 60*s*. to 40*s*. per quarter.

When it is said that 60*s*. is the price of home corn, I presume it is meant that 60*s*. is the natural price—that price which is just sufficient to restore to the English farmer the outgoings necessary to the cultivation of that land which yields no rent, and to pay the usual and ordinary rate of profit.

If this be admitted, it follows, that if the price of corn should fall to 40*s*. per quarter, while other commodities continue at the same prices as before, the worst, or the most unfavourably situated, land can no longer be cultivated, and the ultimate effect must be, that all the land of which the natural fertility is not sufficient to produce one quarter and a half of corn with the same outlay of capital which had previously been required for the production of one quarter, will be thrown out of tillage; and the land so producing one quarter and a half, will then be the worst land in arable cultivation, and will yield no surplus for rent.

A result of this kind is apprehended by many of the agriculturists.

But is it at all probable that this consequence would ensue? Is it not evident that, under the circumstances supposed, the habitual importation of as much corn as is raised upon all the land which produces less than eighteen bushels per acre, would be necessary to produce this consequence, and that the whole of that importation must be effected at 40*s*. per quarter?

But the highest estimate made of the quantity of all kinds of grain which it can be expected would be habitually imported from all parts of the world, in a state of free trade, does not, as far as I know, go beyond three millions of quarters per annum.

Now, three millions of quarters of corn bear so small a proportion to the gross annual produce of the soil (it should be borne in mind that we do not import cattle as well as corn), that even supposing the population to remain stationary, the annual importation of that quantity of foreign grain would not enable us, under the circumstances above stated, to dispense with the tillage of any very considerable extent of inferior land— would not enable us to abandon the cultivation of the poorer soils to such an extent as would reduce the price of home grown corn more than three or four shillings per quarter.

In this argument, I have assumed, for the sake of greater clearness of illustration, that equal quantities of each different quality of soil are brought into cultivation, and that the best land produces twenty-four bushels of corn with the same capital and labour that are required to produce twelve bushels on the worst land. It is probable, however, that the descent from the best to the worst land is not actually in this regular gradation. In the practical application of the principle, it would be necessary to ascertain the ratio of different quantities of land to different qualities. It may be, that in some of the higher steps of the scale, the quantity of land may be of much greater extent than that of the inferior steps. It may be, that the quantity of produce raised upon the worst land, and upon lands approaching to the worst, may be small, compared with the produce of the superior soils. In the former case, the necessity of descending so low in the scale of cultivation might not exist: in the latter, the habitual importation of three millions of quarters of corn might reduce the price of home grown corn considerably more than three or four shillings per quarter.

I might leave the question here, and say, that it is incumbent on those who call for the total removal of all restraint on the importation of foreign corn, or on those who are apprehensive that a free trade in corn would ruin our domestic agriculture, to demonstrate, either that I am mistaken in supposing that the extent to which the price of home grown corn would be affected by the free admission into this country of corn from abroad, would depend, not upon the *cost* of that corn, but upon the *quantity* imported: or, if this cannot be demonstrated, then to show that the quantity imported in a state of free trade would be so large as to satisfy the home demand without the necessity of maintaining in tillage any land which will not produce one hundred and fifty quarters of wheat with the same capital and labour bestowed upon it as are required, under the hypothetical circumstances above stated, to produce one hundred quarters upon land paying no rent.

But there are other important considerations belonging to the question.

It is assumed, in the foregoing statement, that the remunerating price of corn raised at home, under the most unfavourable circumstances, or on that land which pays no rent, is 60*s*., and that foreign corn can be delivered in the home market, after paying freight, insurance, and the charges of importation, at 40*s*.

Now, it is obvious that the continuance of these respective prices for any considerable length of time is impossible: either the price of home-grown corn must fall to the price at which foreign corn can be imported, or the price at which foreign corn can be imported must rise to the price at which home corn can be grown, or the two prices must meet at some intermediate point.

It is important to enquire at what point they would coincide.

This question opens a wide field of enquiry: it involves the consideration of the principles which regulate international commerce, the difference in the value of money in different countries, the effects consequent on variations of the seasons, the ultimate incidence of duties levied upon commodities exported or imported, and the policy and the intention of the former legislation of this country on the trade in corn.

In endeavouring to answer the question, I will adhere to our former supposition, that the prices of home grown corn and of foreign corn are, respectively, 60*s*. and 40*s*. If, under these circumstances, imported corn be admitted duty free, and if, notwithstanding this free admission, the value of money remain the same as before, in other words, if the prices of all commodities of domestic growth and fabric, other than raw produce, remain the same as before, then the price of home grown corn will fall—will fall, probably, at first, below the price at which it will ultimately settle, when the home growth shall have diminished to an extent commensurate with the probable future importations.

But though the price of home corn will fall in consequence of a supply from abroad, yet, as that supply must be inconsiderable compared with the whole of the home demand, and as by far the largest portion of that demand must be supplied by corn of domestic growth, it cannot fall below the price at which that portion of the home grown supply which is raised upon land yielding no rent, can be raised upon such land, with the ordinary rate of agricultural profits.

On the first introduction of foreign corn, the contest must lie between that portion of British corn which is raised at the greatest expense and foreign corn,—including, as to foreign corn, the expense of freight, insurance, &c. The price at which British corn, grown at the geatest expense, can be afforded, is 60*s.*; the price at which foreign corn can be afforded, after paying the expense of carriage, &c. is 40*s.* In the competition the British grower is undersold, and his only remedy is, the removal of that portion of his capital which has ceased to return the ordinary rate of profit, to some other employment. Suppose that before the trade is free, fifty millions of quarters of all kinds of grain are required for the ordinary consumption, that, under these circumstances, the trade is thrown open, and that three millions of quarters are afterwards annually imported from abroad, then, all that capital which had been previously employed in producing three millions of quarters, at home, will be displaced, and the poorest soils on which three millions of quarters had been raised, will be thrown out of tillage.

Suppose, further, that in consequence of falling back upon better land, the natural price of home grown corn (that price which is necessary to restore the capital expended on the poorest soil, and to pay the ordinary rate of profit) should fall to 56*s*., then, although foreign corn can be afforded at 40*s*., yet the importer will be quite willing to take 56*s*. if he can get it, and, under the circumstances supposed, that he would get it, is evident from this consideration, namely, that the whole of the home demand cannot be supplied at a lower price.

The foreign grower would thus get 16*s*. per quarter for his corn more than what is to him a remunerating price.

Now, as the continuance of such a state of things is obviously impossible, the problem to be solved is, in what way the prices of home and of foreign corn would be brought to coincidence, so as not to give to the foreign grower, or to the British importer, a greater rate of profit than the ordinary rate.

It will, perhaps, be said, that as the natural price of foreign corn is 40*s*., the price of home corn will ultimately fall to the price of foreign corn.

Let us examine this point.

Previously to the introduction of foreign corn, a quarter of wheat, raised upon that land which pays no rent is worth 60*s.*; a certain quantity of some other commodity—a cask of nails, for example—is likewise worth 60*s.*; the two commodities are of the same value, and they are so because the money outgoings, together with the ordinary rate of profit upon the capital employed in the production of each, are the same with respect to both. Lessen the money outgoings—lessen the labour and capital necessary to produce the corn, or, which comes to the same thing, increase the quantity of corn produced with the same labour and capital, and, by the ordinary force of competition, the relative value of corn and nails will, in no long time, be altered. But, unless some great improvement in agriculture should take place, the quantity of corn produced with the same labour and capital, can be increased only by raising it on better land.

Now, if in consequence of the importation of foreign corn, we are enabled to fall back upon land of which the natural fertility is so far superior to the worst land now in cultivation as to produce sixty-four quarters and two-sevenths of corn with the same labour and capital that had before been required to produce sixty quarters, then sixty-four quarters and two-sevenths, being the produce of the same money outgoings, will be of the same value as sixty casks of nails.

But sixty casks of nails are worth £180., and therefore, sixty-four quarters and two-sevenths of wheat will likewise be worth £180., or 56*s.* per quarter. If the corn fetch more than 56*s.* per quarter, capital will flow from manufactures to agriculture; if it fetch less than 56*s.*, capital will flow from agriculture to manufactures. It cannot be sold for less than 56*s.* per quarter, and, at the same time, pay the ordinary rate of profit, and yet it has to compete with foreign corn, which, after paying the expense of carriage, and the importing merchant's profit, can be sold at 40*s.* per quarter.

How are we to get rid of this apparent inconsistency? How are the two prices to be brought to coincide? It is said that home corn will fall to the cost at which foreign corn can be imported. Well, let this be admitted, for the sake of the argument. Then I say, that unless it can be shown that there is no tendency to an equalization of profits on capital employed in agriculture and in manufactures, the prices of nails, and of all other commodities of domestic growth and fabric, must fall in the same proportion, that is, in the proportion of 56 to 40.

But such a fall of price is the same thing as a rise in the value of money; and certainly it must be admitted, that if a rise in the value of money be contemplated as one of the results of a free trade in corn, and if that result be brought about to a sufficient extent, the price of home grown corn may fall to the price of foreign corn, consistently with the preservation of an equality of profits in all the different employments of capital in domestic industry.

We can get rid of the inconsistency, then, only by supposing, either that the rate of profit on capital employed in agriculture may be permanently very far below the rate of profit on capital employed in manufactures, or that a free trade in corn will be followed by a very considerable rise in the value of money, or, which comes to the same thing, a great fall in the money prices of all commodities of domestic produce.

It may still, perhaps, be said, that a fall in the price of corn, and of other farm produce, will be attended with a fall in the money wages of agricultural labour, and that such a fall of money wages will enable the British farmer successfully to compete with the foreign grower.

But if the money wages of agricultural labour fall, will not the money wages of manufacturing labour ultimately fall in the same proportion, and for the same reason? And if the farmer, in consequence of diminished money outgoings in the form of wages, can sell his produce at a lower price than before, will not the manufacturer, likewise, and for the same reason, be able to sell his manufactures at lower prices than before?

We cannot, I think, get rid of the inconsistency

in that way. The object contemplated is, a fall in the value of corn, relatively to that of all other things—all other things remaining at the same prices as before—corn falling relatively to them all. Such a fall in the relative value of corn, it appears to me, can be effected only by falling back upon land superior in point of natural fertility to the worst land now in cultivation.

On the supposition, that in a state of free trade in corn we should annually import three millions of quarters of all sorts of grain, I have presumed that we should so far fall back upon soils of superior fertility, as to produce corn at home, on land paying no rent, at 56*s*. per quarter. Imported corn would then sell in the home market at that price. The prices of foreign corn and home corn would thus coincide.

What effect would be produced on the relative value of corn, and of other commodities in the exporting country, we shall have occasion to consider when we come to speak of the value of money in different countries, and the ultimate incidence of duties levied on imported corn. We shall then see that, in consequence of a fall in the value of money in the corn exporting country, the foreign grower will get no greater rate of profit than the ordinary rate.

Mr. Malthus, in his Principles of Political Economy, has put the following case:—

" Let us suppose seven or eight countries, not " very distant from each other, and not very " differently situated with regard to the mines. " Let us suppose, further, that neither their soils " nor their skill in agriculture are essentially " unlike—that their currencies are in a natural " state—their taxes nothing—and that every " trade is free, except the trade of corn. Let us " now suppose one of them greatly to increase in " capital and manufacturing skill above the rest, " and to become, in consequence, much more rich " and populous. I should then say, that this " comparative increase of riches could not possibly " take place without a comparative advance in the " price of raw produce, and that such advance of " price would, under the circumstances supposed, " be the natural sign, and absolutely necessary " consequence, of the increased wealth and popula-" tion of the country in question.

" Let us now suppose the same countries to " have the most perfect freedom of intercourse in " corn, and the expense of freight, &c. to be quite " inconsiderable: and let us still suppose one of " them very greatly to advance above the rest in " wealth and population: I should then say, that " as the importation of corn would prevent any " great difference in the price of raw produce, it " would prevent any great difference in the " quantity of capital laid out upon the land, and " the quantity of corn obtained from it: that, con-

" sequently, the great increase of wealth could not " take place without a great dependence on the " other countries for corn ; and this dependence, " under the circumstances supposed, would be the " natural sign and necessary consequence of the " increased wealth and population of the country " in question."

Let us examine the case thus put by Mr. Malthus.

Previously to the establishment of a free trade in corn among the several countries, the price of corn in all of them is (adopting our former hypothesis) 40*s.* per quarter. One of them now greatly advances in capital and in manufacturing skill, and, in consequence of an increasing demand for corn, its price rises, and it becomes necessary constantly to resort to poorer soils, in order to raise additional produce for an augmenting population. The expense of growing corn being thus increased, the proportionate net return to capital laid out upon the land is diminished, and the relative value of corn to all other commodities, excepting those into which raw produce more or less enters, is raised.

It is thus that a comparatively high price of corn is the necessary accompaniment of an increase of wealth and population.

But what would be the state of things if the trade in corn, as well as all other trades, had been always free ?

Mr. Malthus says, that as the importation of corn would prevent any very great difference in the price of raw produce, it would prevent any very great difference in the quantity of capital laid out upon the land, and the quantity of corn obtained from it.

By this, I presume, it is meant, that agriculture would be pushed in all the several countries, nearly to the same extent; in other words, that the expense of raising raw produce on that land which pays no rent, or under the least favourable circumstances, would be nearly the same in all of them.

But does this necessarily follow? Might not the additional demand for raw produce in the manufacturing country, under the circumstances supposed, be greater than the additional supply which the capital and labour of the poorer countries could produce, over and above their own demand? And would not the quantity of capital laid out upon the land, in that case, be greater, in proportion to the produce raised by it, in the rich than in the comparatively poor countries? If, indeed, the agricultural capital and population of all the several countries were to increase, pari passu, with the increasing demand for raw produce in the manufacturing country, then, certainly, the quantity of capital laid out upon the land would be nearly the same in all, and corn rents, or rents estimated in raw produce, would be nearly the same in all. But that is not the supposition. The case put is, that while one of the countries is greatly increasing in wealth and population, the others remain stationary. In that case, it is impossible that the quantity of capital laid out upon the land should be the same in all the several countries. Not only would the quantity of capital laid out upon the land be greater, but the proportionate net return would be less, in the rich and populous countries, than in those countries that had made little progress in manufacturing industry.

As this is a material point in the argument, it may be well to examine it more closely.

Previously to the start made by one of the several countries in capital and manufacturing skill, the quantity of capital laid out upon the land is supposed to be nearly the same in them all; and as the expense of carriage, &c. is supposed to be quite inconsiderable, the money price of corn must be nearly the same.

One of the countries now greatly increases in wealth and population, and requires, for a greatly augmented number of inhabitants, a great additional quantity of raw produce.

Now, if the capital and population of the neighbouring countries be insufficient to produce, for exportation, any part, or be sufficient to produce only a small part, of this additional quantity, the whole, or the greatest part of it, must be produced in the country requiring it, at an expense gradually increasing with the increase of population and demand.

The price of corn in the prosperous country might thus rise from 40*s*. to 60*s*. per quarter; and as, by the supposition, the expense of carriage, &c. is quite inconsiderable, and the trade in corn free, the same, or nearly the same, price would be obtained in the agricultural as in the manufacturing country. But there would be this important difference, that in the former, money rents would greatly increase, but corn rents would remain nearly the same as before; while in the latter, the rent of land, estimated either in money or in corn, would be greatly augmented.

But it may be said that it is difficult to conceive that while one of several countries, not very distant from each other, is greatly increasing in manufacturing skill, wealth, and population, the others should remain stationary; that it is more probable that the increasing demand for raw produce in the country prospering in manufactures would stimulate the agriculture of its neighbours, and induce an extended and more strenuous cultivation among them.

Well, take the matter in that way. Still, unless the capital and population of the agricultural countries were so far to increase as to enable them to raise a quantity of corn for exportation, and, therefore, over and above what is required for their own subsistence, exactly equal to the additional demand of the manufacturing country, the quantity of capital laid out upon the land, and the proportionate net return to that capital, in the several countries, would not be the same.

Suppose the additional quantity required to be ten millions of quarters of corn, and that three of the ten were imported, and seven produced at home, then, although the price of corn in the several countries would be nearly the same, there would be a considerable difference in the quantity of capital laid out upon the land, and both corn rents and money rents would be higher in the manufacturing than in the agricultural countries.

I have been induced to go into an examination of the case stated by Mr. Malthus in order to show that, with a perfectly free trade in corn, its price may be the same (less the expense of carriage) in the exporting as in the importing country, although the quantity of labour required to produce a given quantity of corn in the two countries may be widely different.

But we may put the case in a different way.

Suppose that, while every trade is free, except the trade in corn, one of the countries greatly increases in wealth and population; that, in consequence of an augmented demand for raw produce, and the necessity of resorting to poorer soils, the price of corn in that country rises from 40*s*. to 60*s*. per quarter, while in the neighbouring countries the price continues at 40*s*. per quarter;

and that, under these circumstances, it is determined to open the ports of the improving country to the free importation of foreign corn, what then will happen?

It appears to me obvious that, in the case supposed, whatever may be the cost of growing corn in the countries which have made no material progress in wealth and population, and in whatever proportions the gross produce of the soil may be divided among labourers, capitalists, and landlords, the price of corn in those countries will very soon rise to its price in the importing country, less the expense of carriage; and that the price at which raw produce will ultimately settle in the importing country will depend on the quantity of corn imported.

In a former statement we have supposed that three millions of quarters of corn are annually imported; that, in consequence of that supply, the natural price of corn in the importing country falls from 60*s*. to 56*s*. per quarter; that the foreign grower obtains that price, and thus, after paying the expense of carriage, &c. obtains 16*s*. per quarter more for his corn than what is to him a remunerating price. But in that statement no allowance was made for the increased cost that would be occasioned in the exporting country by the necessity of resorting to inferior soils to raise the additional quantity of corn required for exportation. If the advance of the exporting country in agriculture were in an inverse proportion to the retrogression of the importing country, that increased cost would be 4*s*. per quarter. Still there would be an excess of 12*s*. per quarter which the foreign grower would get more, for every quarter of corn, than the price at which he can afford to sell it. He would get 56*s*. when the natural price is only 44*s*.

But the foreign farmer would thus get inordinate profits. Such a state of things could not long continue. The money prices of all other commodities produced in the corn exporting country would, in no long time, rise to the new level of the money price of corn, and thus the profits of capital employed in agriculture and manufactures be brought to an equality.

But a general rise of prices is the same thing as a fall in the value of money.

Now, a fall in the value of money, in any country enjoying an extensive commerce, cannot take place without affecting all its commercial dealings with those countries with which it trades: the terms and conditions of its interchange with those countries will all be altered by it.

Hence it becomes important to enquire what is meant by a difference in the value of money in different countries, how it is brought about, and on what it depends.

"When," says Mr. Ricardo, "we speak of the

" high or low value of gold, silver, or any other
" commodity, in different countries, we should
" always mention some medium in which we are
" estimating them, or no idea can be attached to
" the proposition. Thus, when gold is said to be
" dearer in England than in Spain, if no com-
" modity is mentioned, what notion does the as-
" sertion convey? If corn, olives, wine, and wool
" be at a cheaper price in Spain than in England,
" estimated in those commodities, gold is dearer
" in Spain. If, again, hardware, sugar, cloth,
" &c., be at a lower price in England than in
" Spain, then, estimated in those commodities,
" gold is dearer in England. Thus gold appears
" dearer or cheaper in Spain as the fancy of the
" observer may fix on the medium by which he
" estimates its value."

It may, however, be said, that if we fix upon a commodity, the production of which is common to both countries, we shall be able to make a correct estimate of the comparative value of gold and silver in each; or, if we take the money wages of labour in each country as the criterion, we shall be able to form such an estimate. Thus, if the money wages of labour are higher in England than in Spain, then the produce of a given quantity of English labour, of which the wages have been paid in advance, must be worth more gold than the result of the same quantity of Spanish labour, produced under similar circumstances. The difference between the money value of the two products, after making allowance for whatever difference there may be in the rate of profit in each country, must be equal to the difference in the value of money in each.

If the facts of the case could be correctly ascertained—if the average rate of money wages, and the average rate of profit in each country were known—a comparison of the results obtained in this way would certainly indicate the difference of the value of money in the two countries, with reference to their respective powers of production. But we should still want to know how it happens that the money wages of labour are higher in England than in Spain. This it has been attempted to account for by saying, that the superior efficiency and skill with which labour in England is exerted, induce the commercial nations of the world to estimate the produce of a given quantity of English labour more highly in gold and silver than the produce of the same quantity of Spanish labour.

Supposing the correctness of this account of the matter to be admitted, there would still remain another point to be considered, namely, what is the natural limit to the difference in question, and to what variations is it liable?

It appears to me, that some writers of great eminence, in endeavouring to explain this point, have fallen into mistakes which it is important to notice.

In his Elements of Political Economy, Mr. Mill has stated the following supposed case :—

" If two countries can both of them pro-" duce two commodities, corn, for example, and " cloth, but not both commodities with the same " comparative facility, the two countries will find " their advantage in confining themselves, each " to one of the commodities, and bartering for " the other. If one of the countries can produce " one of the commodities with peculiar advan-" tages, and the other the other with peculiar " advantages, the motive is immediately apparent " which should induce each to confine itself to " the commodity which it has peculiar advantages " for producing. But the motive may no less " decidedly exist, where one of the two countries " has facilities superior to the other in producing " both commodities.

" By superior facilities, we mean the power of " producing the same effect with less labour. " The conclusion, too, will be the same, whether " we suppose the labour to be more or less highly " paid. Suppose that Poland, for example, can " produce corn and cloth with less labour than " England, it will not follow that it may not be " the interest of Poland to import one of the " commodities from England. If the degree in " which it can produce with less labour is the " same in both cases ; if, for example, the same " quantity of corn and cloth which Poland can "produce, each with one hundred days' labour, "requires each one hundred and fifty days' labour "in England, Poland will have no motive to "import either from England. But if, while the "same quantity of cloth, which in Poland is pro- "duced with one hundred days' labour, can be "produced in England with one hundred and "fifty days' labour, the facts are such, that "the corn which is produced in Poland with "one hundred days' labour, requires two hun- "dred days' labour in England; in that case, "it will be the interest of Poland to import her "cloth from England. The evidence of these "propositions may thus be traced.

"If the cloth and the corn, each of which "required one hundred days' labour in Poland, "required each one hundred and fifty days' "labour in England, it would follow, that the "cloth of one hundred and fifty days' labour in "England, if sent to Poland, would be equal to "the cloth of one hundred days' labour in Poland; "if exchanged for corn, therefore, it would ex- "change for the corn of only one hundred days' "labour. But the corn of one hundred days' "labour in Poland was supposed to be the same "quantity with that of one hundred and fifty "days' labour in England. With one hundred "and fifty days' labour in cloth, therefore, Eng- "land would only get as much corn in Poland as "she could raise with one hundred and fifty days' "labour at home, and she would, on importing "it, have the cost of carriage besides. In these "circumstances no exchange would take place.

"If, on the other hand, while the cloth pro- "duced with one hundred days' labour in Po- "land was produced with one hundred and fifty "days' labour in England, the corn which was "produced in Poland with one hundred days' "labour could not be produced in England with "less than two hundred days' labour; an "adequate motive to exchange would immediately "arise. With a quantity of cloth which England "produced with one hundred and fifty days' "labour, she would be able to purchase as much "corn in Poland as was there produced with one "hundred days' labour; but the quantity, which "was there produced with one hundred days' "labour, would be as great as the quantity pro- "duced in England with two hundred days' "labour. England, therefore, would obtain her "corn with less labour through the medium of "her cloth.

"Poland would profit in the same manner. A "quantity of corn which cost her one hundred "days' labour, being equal to the quantity pro- "duced in England by two hundred days' la- "bour, would purchase, in England, the produce "of two hundred days' labour in any other com- "modity; for example, in cloth. But the pro- "duce of one hundred and fifty days' labour in

" England, in the article of cloth, is equal to the " produce of one hundred days' labour in Poland. " If, with the produce of one hundred days' " labour, she can purchase, not the produce of " one hundred and fifty, but the produce of two " hundred, she gains to the amount of fifty days' " labour; in other words, a third."

In this statement, Mr. Mill appears to have looked at only one side of the question. His object was, to show what would naturally be the terms and conditions on which exchanges would be made, if the trade between England and Poland were purely a trade of barter. He has supposed that the efficiency and skill with which labour in Poland is exerted, are such, that the cost of raising three quarters of corn is the same as the cost of manufacturing three pieces of cloth; that in England, four pieces of cloth are produced at the same cost as three quarters of corn; and that, therefore, it will be advantageous to England to discontinue the growth of corn, and to exchange cloth for corn with Poland, where three pieces of home made cloth cannot be produced at less cost than three quarters of corn. England will thus get four quarters of corn for four pieces of cloth, less the expense of carriage, &c. instead of producing corn at home, where only three quarters can be produced at the same cost as four pieces.

Thus far, all is clear: it is clear that, whether,

under the circumstance supposed, Poland obtain from England three pieces of cloth in exchange for three quarters of corn, or manufacture the cloth at home, can make no difference, in so far as Poland is concerned; and that England will be a gainer of one quarter of corn by the exchange; in other words, one third.

But Mr. Mill goes on to say, that Poland will profit in the same manner; that it would be advantageous to Poland to discontinue the manufacture of cloth, and to exchange corn for cloth with England, where three quarters of corn cannot be produced at less price than four pieces of cloth. Poland would thus get four pieces of cloth for three quarters of corn, less the expense of carriage, &c. instead of manufacturing cloth at home, where only three pieces can be produced at the same cost as three quarters.

Mr. Mill first says, that by exchanging corn for cloth, Poland will obtain three pieces for three quarters; and then he says that she will obtain four pieces for three quarters. Both propositions cannot be true. The result would probably be, that, under the circumstances supposed, the quantity of cloth given by England to Poland for three quarters of corn would fluctuate between three and four pieces, according to the temporary variations of demand and supply.

But the trade between the two countries is not merely a trade of barter. Exchanges are effected through the medium and intervention of money. Does that intervention alter the nature of the case? I apprehend not. "Gold and silver," says Mr. Ricardo, "having been chosen for the "general medium of circulation, are, by the "competition of commerce, distributed in such "proportions amongst the different countries of "the world as to accommodate themselves to the "natural traffic which would take place if no "such metals existed, and the trade between "different countries were purely a trade of bar-"ter."

Of this proposition Mr. Mill gives the following illustration:—"Suppose the circumstances to be "such in Poland, that, if she produced corn and "cloth for herself, four quarters of corn would have "the same value as ten yards of cloth; of course, "if she had the use of money, the price of four "quarters of corn and ten yards of cloth would be "the same. In England, according to the supposi-"tion, the price of four quarters of corn and that "of twenty yards of cloth would be the same. "There are two supposable cases. The price of "one of the two commodities, corn, for example, "is either equal in the two countries, or not "equal. The illustration of any one of these cases "will suffice for both. Let us, then, suppose that, "in the two countries, the price of corn is equal. If "it is, the price of a yard of cloth must, in Poland, "be twice as great as it is in England. In these

" circumstances, what will happen is obvious: " the cloth, which is cheap in England, will go " to Poland, where it is dear; and there it will " be sold for gold, because there can be no coun- " ter importation of corn, which, by supposition, " is already as cheap in England as in Poland.

" By the importation, in this manner, of English " cloth into Poland, gold goes out of Poland, " and comes into England. The consequence is, " that gold becomes more plentiful in England, " less plentiful in Poland. From this first con- " sequence a second ensues, that prices gradually " rise in England, fall in Poland: the price of " corn, for example, and, along with it, the price " of cloth, rise in England, fall in Poland. If, " when we suppose the traffic to begin, the price " of corn in each country is 1*l*. per quarter, the " price of cloth being, by consequence, in Poland " 8*s*., in England 4*s*. per yard, the supposed " exchange of cloth for gold will gradually, in " England, raise the price of corn above, in " Poland sink it below, 1*l*. per quarter: raise the " price of cloth in England above 4*s*. per yard, " sink it below 8*s*. per yard in Poland. In this " manner, the price of corn in the two countries " gradually recedes from equality, the price of " cloth gradually approaches it. At a certain " point in this progress, corn becomes so dear in " England, and cheap in Poland, that the differ- " ence of price will pay for the cost of carriage.

"At that moment a motive arises for the impor-
"portation of corn into England; and prices
"regulate themselves in such a manner, that in
"England corn is dearer than in Poland, by the
"expense of carrying corn; cloth is dearer in
"Poland than in England, by the expense of
"carrying cloth, from the one country to the
"other. At this point, the value of the cloth
"imported into the one country, and that of the
"corn imported into the other, balance one
"another. The exchange is then at par, and
"gold ceases to pass."

In this Mr. Mill appears to have fallen into the same error as in the former case. There is no better reason for concluding that, under the circumstances supposed, the price of cloth in England will rise only a little above 4*s*. per yard, and thus enable Poland to obtain nearly twenty yards of cloth for four quarters of corn, than for concluding that cloth will fetch nearly 8*s*. per yard in Poland, and thus enable England to obtain nearly eight quarters of corn for twenty yards of cloth. Poland can afford to give, in the way of barter, eight quarters of corn for twenty yards of cloth. England can afford to take four quarters of corn for twenty yards of cloth. The result would probably be, that the terms of the interchange would fluctuate between these extremes, and that money prices would adjust themselves accordingly.

I have deemed it right to state at length, and in his own words, the cases which Mr. Mill has put. This I have done in order to mark the error into which a very acute mind appears, on this subject, to have fallen.

The case may be more commodiously and more concisely stated as follows.

England can produce four yards of cloth at the same cost of labour as that at which she can produce one quarter of corn : Poland can produce only three yards of cloth at the same cost of labour as that at which she can produce one quarter of corn. Before the traffic between the two countries begins, the price of corn in England is 60*s*. per quarter, in Poland 40*s*. per quarter. The price of cloth in England is 15*s*. per yard, in Poland 20*s*. per yard. Under these circumstances the people of England say, "Open the trade with Poland, and we shall be able to buy corn at 40*s*. per quarter, and to sell our cloth at 20*s*. per yard." The people of Poland say, "Open the trade with England, and we shall be able to sell our corn at 60*s*. per quarter, and to buy cloth at 15*s*. per yard." It is obvious that both parties cannot be right in their anticipations, and the question is, at what point the barter of cloth for corn, and the prices accommodated to that barter, will settle on the opening of the trade. I apprehend that the point will depend on this circumstance, namely, whether the demand in England for corn is so strong as to raise the price of corn in Poland from 40*s*. to 60*s*. per quarter; or the demand in Poland for cloth so strong as to raise the price of cloth in England from 15*s*. to 20*s*. per yard. If the former, then Poland will obtain three yards of cloth in exchange for one quarter of corn; if the latter, then England will obtain from Poland one quarter and half of corn for three yards of cloth. In both cases allowance must be made for the expense of carrying the cloth and the expense of carrying the corn. The probability is, that the barter point would shift and vary between the extremes above mentioned.

To simplify the question, I have supposed the trade between the two countries to be confined to the exchange of cloth for corn; but not only are there many other commodities which enter into such a trade, but each country has commercial dealings with other countries, which dealings must indirectly affect their trade with each other, and prevent so great an effect being produced as is above described. Generally, however, it is true, as is stated by Mr. Ricardo, that gold and silver are distributed amongst the commercial nations of the world in such proportions as to render the traffic carried on between them purely a trade of barter; and that, if any one of them possesses peculiar facilities for the production of any commodity that is universally the object of demand, the general prices of that country will be on a higher scale than that of the countries with which it deals, *unless* those countries possess a like facility in the production of some other commodity which is equally the object of universal demand, in which case the peculiar advantage of the first mentioned country will, in a greater or less degree, be counteracted.

The great improvements made in manufacturing skill, within the last half century, have given to this country an advantage of this nature: the price of labour, and consequently the prices of all commodities of domestic growth and fabric, are upon a higher scale in Great Britain than in the countries with which it has commercial dealings; in other words, the value of gold and silver, estimated in labour, is lower in Great Britain than in most parts of the world.

Connected with this part of the enquiry there is an important consideration, which it is material to notice.

We have seen that a country possessing peculiar facilities in the production of a commodity universally in demand, acquires a higher scale of general prices than that of neighbouring countries with which it deals; and that this higher scale of prices will be brought about, in the first instance, by an extraordinary importation of the precious metals. Thus, if before the peculiar facility is acquired, England imports twenty pipes of wine from Portugal, at £50. per pipe, and exports to Portugal twenty bales of cloth, at £50. per bale, the transactions balance, and the exchange between the two countries is at par.

England now, in consequence of improved skill, and the aid of new machinery, is able to produce one hundred bales with the same expenditure of labour that had previously been required for the production of fifty bales, and the price of cloth, in consequence of this increased facility of production, falls—not in the proportion of 100 to 50, but—say from £50. to £40. per bale, and the demand of Portugal, at the reduced price, from twenty to thirty bales; while the demand of England for the wine of Portugal remains the same as before. Every transaction in commerce is an independent transaction. The merchant who exported the cloth to Portugal is paid for it with Portuguese money, and with that money purchases a bill of exchange for £1,200. on England. The seller of the bill, finding that he can obtain a counter bill in the market only for £1,000., and knowing that he must send £200. in gold to England, in order to settle these transactions, demands such a price for the bill of £1,200. as will cover the expense of transmitting gold to England, together with his fair and usual profit; in other words, the exchange is against Portugal, and gold flows into England.

By the abstraction of gold from Portugal, and

the accumulation of it in England, prices are lowered in Portugal, and raised in England, until the increased demand for wine in England, at a reduced price, brings the transaction between the two countries to a balance: the exchange is again at par, and gold ceases to pass. Now, the circumstance to which I wish to call your attention is this: if the favoured country has the use of paper money, then, instead of importing gold, under the circumstances supposed, that country may enlarge its circulation of paper. The effect to be produced is, an alteration of the *relative* prices of the two countries. Suppose the alteration to be produced is 10 per cent., then, whether prices are raised 5 per cent. in the one, and lowered 5 per cent. in the other, or remain stationary in the one, and rise 10 per cent. in the other, it comes, in so far as relative prices are concerned, to the same thing.

Now, general prices may be as effectually raised by an augmentation of paper as by an augmentation of gold. Under the circumstances supposed, there may, therefore, take place an augmentation of the paper circulation in the favoured country, without depressing the foreign exchange below the par level. This subject cannot be better expressed than in the words of Mr. Ricardo:—" This higher value of money will not " be indicated by the exchange; bills may con- " tinue to be negociated at par, although the "prices of corn and labour should be 10, 20, or "30 per cent. higher in one country than another. "Under the circumstances supposed, such a "difference of prices is the natural order of "things, and the exchange can only be at par "when a sufficient quantity of money is introduced "into the country excelling in manufactures, so "as to raise the price of its corn and labour. "If foreign countries should prohibit the exporta-"tion of money, and could successfully enforce "obedience to such a law, they might indeed "prevent the rise in the prices of the corn and "labour of the manufacturing country; for such "rise can only take place after the influx of the "precious metals, supposing paper money not to "be used; but they could not prevent the ex-"change from being very unfavourable to them. "If England were the manufacturing country, "and it were possible to prevent the importation "of money, the exchange with France, Holland, "and Spain might be 5, 10, or 20 per cent. "against those countries.

"Whenever the current of money is forcibly "stopped, and when money is prevented from "settling at its just level, there are no limits to "the possible variations of the exchange. The "effects are similar to those which follow when a "paper money, not exchangeable for specie at the "will of the holder, is forced into circulation.

"Such a currency is necessarily confined to the "country where it is issued: it cannot, when too "abundant, diffuse itself generally amongst other "countries. The level of circulation is destroyed, "and the exchange will inevitably be unfavour-"able to the country where it is excessive in "quantity: just so would be the effects of a "metallic circulation, if by forcible means, by "laws which could not be evaded, money should "be detained in a country, when the stream of "trade gave it an impetus towards other coun-"tries."

We may now return to the main points involved in this enquiry.

I have supposed, in a former statement, that in this country the natural price of corn, raised upon that land, or rather, with that capital, which pays no rent, is 60*s*. per quarter, and that foreign corn, after paying the expenses of importation, can be afforded at 40*s*. per quarter. What proportion of the difference between the two prices is to be attributed to difficulty of production, and what to a difference in the value of money, can be matter only of conjecture. Mr. Malthus was of opinion, that of the very great difference between the price of corn in England and Bengal, the largest part is owing to a difference in the value of money in the two countries;

and that the greater part of the high price of corn in this country, compared with most of the states of Europe, is occasioned in the same way. In order to fix our ideas, in this respect, let us suppose, that of the difference between the two prices of 60*s.* and 40*s.*, ten shillings are occasioned by difficulty of production, and ten shillings by a difference in the value of money, it would then follow that the scale of general prices is 20 per cent. higher, in other words, that gold is 20 per cent. lower in this, than in those countries from which corn can be imported at 40*s.* per quarter. These points being settled, we have to consider what effect the value of money, in this and the corn exporting country, would be produced, by opening the ports to the free admission of foreign corn.

I have already endeavoured to show, that if, under the circumstances which I have supposed, we should habitually import three millions of quarters of grain yearly, we might so far fall back upon land of superior fertility as to produce corn at home, with that capital which pays no rent, at 56*s.* per quarter; and that the corn exporting countries would so far advance upon inferior soils, as to increase the money cost of growing corn abroad 4*s.* per quarter. There would still be a difference of 12*s.* between the foreign and the home price. How is that difference to be extinguished? It appears to me, that if a perfectly free trade in corn were established the difference in question could be extinguished only by a new distribution of the precious metals, or such a contraction of the paper circulation of this country as would occasion a general fall of prices of all commodities of domestic growth and fabric.

I have observed, that the foreign price of corn must rise to the English price, or the English price must fall to the foreign price, or the two prices must meet at some intermediate point. If the importing price should rise to the price at which the English corn can be grown, that is, to 56*s*. per quarter, then the money wages of labour, and of all commodities in the corn exporting country, must rise in the same proportion. But such a rise of general prices cannot take place without an increase in the quantity of money.

The result, I apprehend, would be, a fall in the foreign exchange in this country, and a continuance of the depression until a new level of general prices has been effected.

We may now perceive where, on the suppositions on which I have proceeded, a duty levied on the importation of foreign corn must ultimately fall.

We have seen that, by allowing foreign corn to be imported, duty free, the foreign grower will get 12*s*. per quarter more for his corn than the price at which, according to the existing scale of general prices, in his own country, he can afford to sell it. If, then, a duty, less than 12*s*. were levied on imported corn, a portion of the 12*s*. would be intercepted, or, which comes to the same thing, the duty would ultimately fall on the foreign grower.

The legislation of this country appears to have proceeded on the belief, that it is possible to regulate the price of corn by a varying scale of duties levied on its importation. Permanently to control and determine the price in that way appears to me to be impracticable.

I am aware it may be said, that if foreign corn were admitted duty free, or if the duty levied on its importation were small, the quantity of corn imported would be much larger than it would be if a high duty were levied.

I can admit this proposition only to this extent, namely, that if the duty were small, corn might be imported from places more distant, and less advantageously situated for exportation, than if the duty were high; the difference between a high and a small duty being, in a great measure, absorbed, as to those places, by the greater expense and risk of transportation.

In submitting to you the foregoing observations on the importation of foreign corn, I pretend to no peculiar knowledge of facts and circumstances, but offer them only as an attempt to illustrate the principles with reference to which, it appears to me, this subject ought to be considered.

I remain,

My dear Sir,

Ever faithfully yours,

JAMES PENNINGTON.

CURRENCY AND COINAGE.

"The too great facility of expansion at one time, and the "too rapid contraction of paper credit (I speak of it in the "largest sense) at another, is unquestionably an evil of the "greatest magnitude. To devise a safe remedy, and to "apply it when found, are not easy tasks in the present "artificial state of this country, and with a due regard to all "the great interests at stake.

"This, for a long time, has appeared to me one of the "most important matters that can engage the attention of "the legislature, and the councils of the country."

Letter from Mr. Huskisson.

An enquiry into the state of the currency involves the consideration of the following questions:—

Of what does the medium of interchange, in the metropolis and in the provinces, practically consist?

In what way, and to what extent, are the prices of commodities, the rate of interest, and the foreign exchange, affected by variations in its amount, and by the manner in which it is employed?

First,—The circulating medium of the metropolis.

This consists of the gold and silver coins of the realm, of the notes of the Bank of England, and of the transferrable book-debts of seventy or eighty banking establishments, which book-debts are payable on demand, in Bank of England notes, or in coin.

These may be considered in their order.

I. The gold and silver coins of the realm.

Previous to the year 1798, the mint was open to the public for the coinage of both gold and silver, at certain specified rates, namely, of gold at the rate of £3. 17*s.* 10½*d.*, and of silver at the rate of 5*s.* 2*d.* per ounce. But, before that period, the price of silver having been higher in the market than at the mint, very little silver was brought to the mint to be coined. It is stated by Lord Liverpool, in his treatise on the coins of the realm, that from the year 1699, when the great recoinage was completed, to the end of the year 1717, no more than £674,831. 15*s.* 9*d.*, in tale, was coined; and of this sum, £320,372. 12*s.* were ancient Scottish silver coins, or foreign coins permitted to be current in Scotland before the Union; which pieces were recoined at Edinburgh into coins of the English standard, by virtue of the Treaty of Union. Two other parts of this sum, that is, £78,811. 6*s*., coined in the year 1709, and £76,780. 16*s*., coined in the year 1711, were principally made of plate, brought to the mint in consequence of special encouragements then given. From the plate so brought in, £144,000. was converted into coin; and only £115,92. 2*s*. was coined from silver bullion brought into the mint, in the usual course, during these two years; so that the natural or ordinary coinage of silver, during this period of eighteen years, amounted to no more than £210,459. 3*s*. 9*d*.

Lord Liverpool appears to have thought, that this indisposition of the public to bring silver to the mint was owing to a preference, by the people, of gold to silver. He observes that, "in very "rich countries, especially those in which great "and extensive commerce is carried on, gold is "the most proper metal of which the principal "measure of property, and instrument of com- "merce, should be made. In such countries, gold "will become, in practice, the principal measure "of property, and instrument of commerce, not "only without the support of law, but in spite of "almost any law that can be enacted to the con- "trary; for the principal purchases and ex- "changes cannot there be made, with any con- "venience, in coins of a less valuable metal."

Notwithstanding the deference justly due to this high authority, it may be doubted whether the inferences contained in the above cited passage are strictly correct. It is, at least, certain, that if, in any country, however opulent it may be, and however extensive and multifarious its commerce, the denominative proportion of silver to gold be higher in the market than at the mint, and coins of both metals be made a legal tender at their mint denominations, only the former will be brought there for coinage. The inconvenience of its bulk would, in all probability, be obviated by the issue of mint notes, against deposits of silver, or by the establishment of banks of deposit and of transfer, similar to the celebrated banking establishments of Hamburgh and Amsterdam.

When the recoinage of 1696-9 was completed, the guinea, the value of which had been reduced by act of Parliament to 22*s.*, fell, without any interposition of authority, to 21*s.* 6*d.* This fall did not bring the value of the two metals, relatively to each other, to the proportion which obtained in the market. Silver, relatively to gold, was still estimated at the mint lower than it ought to have been. The consequence was, that the new silver coinage, amounting to £6,882,908. 17*s.* 7*d.*, was, in a short time, melted down and exported. In the year 1717 the value of the guinea was lowered, by proclamation, to 21*s.*, and other gold coins in proportion. Notwithstanding this reduction, gold, in reference to silver, was still estimated in the market lower than at the mint, and so continued until the year 1798, by which time the price of silver had so far fallen as to induce some individuals to bring silver to the mint, for the purpose of being coined at the rate of 5*s.* 2*d.* per ounce. If this coinage had been suffered to proceed, the gold coins would, in their turn, have been melted down and exported. To prevent this consequence, the act of 38 Geo. III., cap. 59, was passed, by which the further coinage of silver was suspended.

In the year 1816 the 56 Geo. III., cap. 60, was passed, by which it is enacted, that, after a day to be appointed by proclamation, silver coin and bullion may be brought to the mint to be coined, at the rate of 66*s.* per lb., troy weight, and that the silver so coined shall be a legal tender, to the extent of 40*s.* As no proclamation to this effect has been issued, the public are precluded from availing themselves of the permission granted by the act; and no silver has since been coined at the mint without the express permission and authority of government.

It thus appears that, in consequence of the over-valuation of the gold coins in 1717, and the exclusion of the public from the silver department of the mint since the year 1798, the gold currency of this country has formed the bulk of its specie, for more than a century past; and that, during the whole of that period, neither in pecuniary contracts at home, nor in our commercial intercourse with foreign countries, has the mint price of 5*s*. 2*d*. per ounce for silver been practically referred to.

It is no valid objection to this conclusion to say, that, by the 14 Geo. III., passed in 1774, silver coins were a legal tender, by weight, to any amount, and so continued until the year 1783, when the act expired. At that period, the silver coins in circulation were so much reduced by wear, that payment by weight, could not have been made without great loss. The enactment, therefore, was nugatory. It is true, indeed, that before the year 1798, it was competent to any one to bring silver to the mint to be coined, and, by so doing, to discharge his money obligations with silver, at the rate of 5*s*. 2*d*. per ounce; but, for the reasons already stated—namely, the higher price of silver in the market than at the mint—no one, without considerable disadvantage, could avail himself of that privilege.

Hence it appears, that gold, at the rate of £3. 17*s*. 10½*d*. per ounce, has been the sole practical measure of property, and of exchange, in this country, for more than a hundred years; and that the silver coins in circulation are subsidiary and subordinate to the gold coins, and are upheld in their value on a level with that of the gold coin, by the limitation of their quantity.

No seignorage is charged by the mint upon the gold coins; nor would it be practicable, under the system of currency which obtains in this country, to subject the principal measure of property to a charge of this nature.

In order to explain this point, it is necessary to advert to the principles, and the operation, of mint regulations.

When a seignorage, or mint charge, is taken, the value of the coins in circulation ought to exceed the value of the metal of which they are made, by a sum equal to the value of the seignorage, together with that of the loss they may have sustained by wear. Only so long as they do so, will the metal of which they are made be brought by the public to the mint.

There are four ways, in any of which this excess of value may be destroyed.

First,—By false and illegal coinage.

Second,—By the purchase and coinage of gold and silver by government, according to the practice of the mints of France.

Third,—By the issue of paper money.

Fourth,—By an unfavourable foreign exchange.

With respect to the first of the causes here enumerated, it may be observed that, although it cannot be wholly prevented by the dread of punishment, yet, unless other causes of depression are simultaneously in operation, it is not likely to prevail to a very serious extent. It is most likely to come into operation when the coins in circulation are materially injured by wear and clipping. The practice of weighing and examining the coins conduces to the prevention of it.

The second cause of depression is necessarily very slight, and depends altogether upon the discretion of the officers of the mint.

The third and fourth involve questions of considerable importance. When the issue of paper money is restrained by no other check than the obligation to pay it on demand in coin, it will always be the interest, and, therefore, the practice, of the issuers to extend the circulation of it as far as is possible, consistent with the due observance of the obligation. "If the seignorage of gold coin were 5 per cent., for instance, the currency might be really depreciated 5 per cent. before it would be the interest of the holders to demand coin, for the purpose of melting it into bullion." The excess of the market over the mint price of gold, and the unfavourable state of the foreign exchange, at the accession of George III., have commonly been attributed to the worn and imperfect state of the coins at that time in circulation. It may be doubted, however, whether that cause alone was sufficient to produce the effect complained of. If no paper money had at that time existed, the worn and injured coins would, it is probable, have been sustained in their original value by the limitation of their quantity, and no material excess of the market, over the mint price, of gold, nor any depression of the foreign exchange, have been experienced. The wear and deterioration of the coins would have been regarded in the light of an accidental seignorage. For the same reason, it is probable that if the Bank of France were to issue notes of so low a denomination as 100 francs, and banks of circulation were established in all the principal departments of France, the silver coins in circulation would, in no long time, be deprived of that excess of value which they now possess as coin over their value as bullion, and that silver would no longer be brought, by government, or the public, to the mint for coinage. The coins of that metal would, in that event, gradually become more and more debased by wear and clipping: all the evils of an unsound and uncertain currency would be experienced, and no remedy for it be found but in the trouble and vexation of an expensive recoinage.

In England, so long as the present system of currency is continued, effects similar to those above described would, it is probable, result from a seignorage, or mint charge. It cannot, therefore, with propriety, be taken. The coins into which the paper money is convertible can properly be issued from the mint at no greater value than that of the metal of which they are made; and the mint can, with safety, be open to the public for the coinage of one metal only.

An unfavourable foreign exchange might, in

the absence of all other causes of depression, lessen, or altogether destroy, the augmented value created by a seignorage. If, when the mint charge upon gold coins is 1 per cent., the foreign exchange should fall 1½ per cent., it would be profitable to export the coins. The value of the coins and that of the metal contained in them would, in that case, coincide.

This cause of depression, however, in the absence of other causes, is not likely to be of frequent occurrence, or of long continuance. It is well observed by Mr. Huskisson, that "the "operations of the trade of bullion originate "almost wholly in the fresh supplies which are "yearly poured in from the mines of the New "World, and are chiefly confined to the distri- "bution of those supplies through the different "parts of Europe. If this supply were to cease "altogether, the dealings in gold and silver, as "objects of trade, would be very few, and those "of short duration."

From the foregoing observations it appears that, under the present system of the English currency, a seignorage upon the principal coins cannot, with propriety, be taken, and that the issue of the subsidiary coins is properly restrained by the discretion of the government. If silver were to become the principal measure of value, it would, in like manner, be necessary to issue gold coins at a higher denomination than their worth expressed in terms of the silver coins, and to limit their amount; or to issue them at a lower denomination than their worth in the silver coins, and to allow them to be bought and sold at an agio, or premium.

Hence, likewise, it follows, that the adoption of a silver standard would be impracticable, without a depreciation of the metallic currency; for, unless the mint were open to the public for the coinage of silver at a higher denomination than corresponds with the nominal value of the gold coins now in circulation, the supremacy of the silver coins could not be effectually established.

According to the present regulation of the British mint, gold is the ultimate standard to which all money contracts have reference. The sovereign, when first issued from the mint, should weigh 5 dwts. 3.274 grains. By a proclamation dated 6th February, 1821, the current weight was fixed at 5 dwts. 2½ grains, or $\frac{628}{1000}$ per cent. below the standard weight. When reduced, by wear or otherwise, below 5 dwts. 2½ grains, the sovereign is no longer a legal tender.

Putting aside, for the present, the question of depreciation, the principal ground for advocating a change from a gold to a silver standard is the alteration which was made in the mint law of the United States of America in the year 1834. That alteration will, it may be expected, occasion a considerable demand upon the rest of the world for gold, which demand, although it may occasionally be suspended by commercial difficulties, will, it is probable, in the long run prevail. Previous to the year 1834, the mint proportion of silver to gold, in the United States, was as fifteen to one. As this was lower than the market proportion, very little gold was brought by the public to the mint; and the metallic money of the United States consisted almost wholly of silver. By the mint regulations of 1834, an eagle of the new coinage, containing 232 grains of fine gold, is declared to be equal to ten dollars; and as a dollar contains $371\frac{1}{4}$ grains of fine silver, silver to gold is rated, at the American mint, in the proportion of sixteen to one.

In England (assuming the value of silver $\frac{222}{240}$ fine, to be 5*s*. per ounce, expressed in terms of gold, $\frac{220}{240}$ fine, at £3 17*s*. $10\frac{1}{2}$*d*. per ounce), the proportion is 15.71 to 1.

In France, the mint proportion, since the 1st July, 1835, has been 15.65 to 1: the market proportion is generally a small fraction higher.

In the general market of Europe, it is probable that the proportion is 15.71 to 1.

Assuming this to be the case, let us see what is the necessary effect of the new mint regulations of the United States upon the exchange between that country and Europe.

We have seen, that, according to those regulations, 100 grains of fine gold are deemed equal to 1600 grains of fine silver; or, which comes to the same thing, that sixteen eagles, containing 3712 grains of fine gold, will discharge a debt of the same amount as 160 dollars, containing 594,000 grains of fine silver. But in Europe, 594,000 grains of fine silver are worth 3781 grains, of fine gold. In the United States, therefore, it has become the interest of every banker, merchant, and trader, to convert the silver dollars in his possession into gold, to send them to Europe for that purpose, and to discharge his money obligations, at home, with gold rather than with silver. By so doing, he will save about one and half per cent. This, it may be said, is hardly sufficient to compensate the risk and expense of transmitting silver to Europe and receiving gold in return. That is true; but then it should be recollected that, in the ordinary course of their commercial dealings with Europe, the merchants of the United States have frequent occasion to export and import the precious metals. Previous to the year 1834, those exports and imports consisted mainly of silver. It may now be expected that the exports will consist mainly of silver, and the imports mainly of gold.

It may, indeed, be said, that the necessity for silver coins in small payments, will cause them to be retained in the country.

That this necessity will induce a considerable circulation of silver in the country, there can be no doubt; but, unless the government of the United States should again alter its mint regulations, those silver coins will not be Mexican nor United States dollars. Much inconvenience in this respect, will, it is to be apprehended, hereafter be experienced; and it is probable, that, in order to obviate that inconvenience, the government of the United States will be obliged to resort to the expedient which has been successfully adopted in Great Britain, namely, that of rendering their silver coins subsidiary and subordinate to the gold coins. In the mean time, the business of exchanging the silver coins now circulating in the United States, for the gold of Europe, will be carried on whenever the exportation and importation of specie shall become necessary or expedient.

Now, as the basis of the currency of Great Britain is gold, and as the great extent of the commercial dealings between the United States and Great Britain will naturally direct a large share of the American demand for gold towards this country, the advocates for a silver standard may say, that the occasional pressure of this demand would be averted, or at least mitigated, by the adoption of silver as the basis of the currency.

The answer to this argument is, that, according to the present value of the two metals, relatively to each other, in the general market of the world, such an alteration would be impracticable without a depreciation of the metallic standard; and that, if the value of silver should materially fall, relatively to gold, the alteration would not accomplish the object proposed by it.

The Notes of the Bank of England.

In the report of the Committee of Public Expenditure, in 1807, it is observed, that "a note "holder does not essentially differ from a person "to whom a balance is due. Both are creditors "of the bank; the one holding a note which is "the evidence of the debt due to him, the other "having the evidence in the ledger of the bank."

The following questions were put to Mr. Simon Martin, by the Committee on Joint Stock Banks, in 1836.

"With regard to the circulation of bank notes, "do you think it makes any material difference "in the power of the bank to afford accommodation, either discreetly or indiscreetly, whether it "issues promissory notes?"

"I think that the issuing promissory notes in a "manufacturing district, where profits are small, "affords useful accommodation; but with us it is "nothing, compared with the extent of our "deposits."

"Would it materially prevent a bank giving "this indiscreet stimulus to trade, to which you "have alluded, if they did not issue notes? or

" are there means of rediscounting, or otherwise, " by which they might give it without?"

" According to my feeling on the subject, it " avails them but very little. I will give my " notion of the theory of a bank circulation. I " consider the circulation of country bank notes " of issue to be this : it never could be permanent " unless founded on bank notes, or their equiva- " lent. *A country bank note is, in fact, but a " circulated deposit voucher.* The bank issuing " that stands debtor to the bearer, by number, " instead of to A. B. on account."

The account given by the Parliamentary Committee of 1807, and by Mr. Simon Martin in his evidence, of the essential identity of a deposit and a bank note, is undoubtedly correct; but there is this important difference in the practical employment and application of them, that, in the case of the Bank of England, and likewise in that of the country banks, a deposit, or a credit in the ledger of the bank, is not commonly used as the medium of interchange until it is converted into a promissory note.

In the metropolis, the notes of the Bank of England are employed as a substitute for, and perform the functions of, metallic money. The principle on which they are issued, and the circumstances by which the amount of the issue is ultimately controlled and limited, we shall have occasion to consider hereafter. In the mean while, it may not be improper to advert to an opinion on the subject of the paper issues of the metropolis which has been asserted, and which is still not without its advocates.

It has been said, and it is still occasionally contended, that to confine the issue of paper money to a single body is an undue interference with the freedom of trade, which interference cannot but be frequently injurious; that if the business of issue in the metropolis were open to the competition of joint stock companies, the practice which would, doubtless, prevail, of daily exchanging their notes with each other, would prevent any imprudent or excessive issue; that the self-interest of the banks would always ensure a sufficient circulation; and that the public would thus be equably supplied with the precise quantity of paper money which the wants and the convenience of commerce require.

In reply to these pretensions, it may be asked, Of what—if the freedom contended for were permitted—if various banks of issue in the metropolis were established—of what would the reserved cash of those banks practically consist? of Bank of England notes or of coin? Chiefly, it is probable, of the former; especially if the Bank of England continued to be (as in all probability it would) the principal bank of issue in the metropolis. If so, then, upon the Bank of England would rest the responsibility, not only of controlling the circulation of all the other banks, but of keeping in reserve a sufficient quantity of metallic money to supply, not only the internal wants of the country with coin, but likewise every demand for bullion for exportation.

And what advantage would the public derive from this competition? The notes of the new banks—if they obtained circulation at all—would not be of *superior* credit to those of the Bank of England. Only a certain quantity of paper, by whomsoever issued, can be sustained consistently with the maintenance of its value on a level with that of the legal coin of the realm. The public, then (whatever might be the advantage or profit to the banks themselves), would derive no advantage from conceding to them the privilege contended for. On the contrary, it is probable that, upon every occasion of commercial excitement, the issue of the banks collectively would be unduly extended, and that at every period of depression, whether originating in mercantile discredit, or in an extraordinary demand for metallic money for domestic purposes or for exportation, the fears and the conflicts of the rival banks would lead to an inconvenient, if not a disastrous, contraction of their issues.

Neither the security nor the advantage of the public, then, would be promoted by the change, but on the contrary, would be exposed to the risk of severe and dangerous vicissitudes.

With respect to undue interference with the freedom of trade, Dr. Adam Smith has justly observed, "To restrain private people, it may be "said, from receiving in payment the promissory "notes of a banker, for any sum great or small, "when they themselves are willing to receive "them; or to restrain a banker from issuing such "notes, when all his neighbours are willing to "accept of them, is a manifest violation of that "natural liberty which it is the proper business "of law not to infringe but to support. Such "regulations may, no doubt, be considered as, in "some respects, a violation of natural liberty. "But those exertions of the natural liberty of "a few individuals which might endanger the "security of the whole society are, and ought to "be, restrained by the laws of all governments— "of the most free as well as the most despotic. "The obligation of building party walls, in order "to prevent the communication of fire, is a viola-"tion of natural liberty, exactly of the same kind "with the regulations of the banking trade."

Transferable Book Debts of the London Bankers.

It has been questioned whether these, or any part of them, can properly be considered as forming part of the circulation; and as this point is one of material importance, it is desirable that it should be carefully examined.

In order to determine the question it is necessary to advert to the nature of those obligations, and to the manner in which they are employed.

They are payable on demand in Bank of England notes or in coin.

It is not, however, solely on this account, and because they may be drawn for at will, and thus give the command of a corresponding amount of bank notes, that they constitute a part of the circulating medium, but because a large proportion of them is employed in effecting purchases and payments without being first converted into the medium in which they are payable. In a large majority of instances, the holder of a cheque upon a banker, instead of demanding bank notes for the cheque, is contented to hold the amount of the cheque in the form of a book debt of that or of some other banker, which book debt may be again transferred to a third person, and so on, indefinitely, without being first converted into either bank notes or coin.

When the book debts of a banker are thus transferred from one person to another without being first converted into the cash in which they are payable, they are used as the medium of interchange exactly on the same principle as that on which a bank note is so used without being first converted into the coin which it promises to pay.

It may, perhaps, be said, that although the book debts, or credit of any kind, may be used as the means of adjusting transactions, yet those debts, or that credit, when so employed, can be regarded only as an auxiliary currency, employed for the purpose of facilitating those adjustments; that even admitting that the book debts of bankers are largely used in effecting purchases and payments, such an employment of them can be considered only as one of the means of economizing the use of bank notes; that this economy is a matter which concerns only the bankers themselves; that, whether a cheque upon a banker is discharged with bank notes, or by the transfer of a book debt into the name of the holder of the cheque, can make no difference to the drawer of the cheque; that the object of the latter will have been attained, if the party to whom he has given a cheque be at liberty to exercise his pleasure and discretion as to whether he shall receive bank notes for the cheque, or the transferable book debt of a banker; that the question is one merely of terms, and must be solved by a strict definition of the terms employed, rather than by a long argument, conducted in expressions of doubtful meaning.

This explanation will hardly appear satisfactory to those who, in order to test its accuracy, apply it to a state of things which, although not immediately probable, is certainly very possible. Such persons may say, Let it be supposed that all merchants, traders, and other persons in the metropolis, have opened drawing accounts at the Bank of England; that the bank has established stations in different parts of London and Westminster for the convenience of the depositors; that all payments of five pounds, and upwards, are made by cheques upon the bank; that all payments under five pounds are made, as at present, with metallic money: then, as there would be no bank notes, and as the transferable book debts of the bank, payable in specie on demand, would be the only medium of interchange in the metropolis, in all transactions of the value of five pounds and upwards, those transferable book debts (bank deposits) would be, not merely the auxiliary, but the principal currency of the metropolis.

If it be replied, that this is not the actual state of things; that the business of banking in London, instead of being confined to a single bank, is conducted by seventy or eighty different bankers; and that a large proportion of the money transactions of the metropolitan district is effected by means of bank notes, by those who do, and a still larger proportion by those who do not, keep an account open with a banker;—if this reply be urged, still it may be contended that the actual state of things differs from the supposed case only in degree; and that to solve the question really at issue, it is only necessary to ascertain what portion of the transferable book debts of the seventy or eighty banking establishments is used in effecting purchases and payments, without being first converted into the bank notes or coin in which they are payable.

Now, it appears by the evidence of the Inspector of the Clearing House, before the Bullion Committee of 1810, that the average amount of drafts paid there daily, at that time, was £4,700,000., and that the average balance paid in bank notes was no more than £220,000.

Since the year 1810, the average amount of daily payments at the Clearing House, has, no doubt, greatly increased, and it is probable that the average amount of bank notes required for their liquidation has not increased in the same proportion.

The process of clearing is described by Mr. Henry Thornton, in the following terms:—

" It is the practice of each of the London " bankers to send a clerk, at an agreed hour in " the afternoon, to a room provided for their use. " Each clerk there exchanges the drafts on other " bankers received at his own house, for the " drafts on his own house received at the houses " of other bankers. The balances of the several " bankers are transferred in the same room from " one to another, and the several balances are " finally wound up by each clerk into one balance: " the difference between the whole sum which " each banker has to pay to all other city bankers, " and the whole sum which he has to receive of

" all other city bankers, is therefore all that is " discharged, in bank notes or money."

It thus appears, that a very large proportion of the funds lodged in the hands of the private bankers of the metropolis is employed as the medium of interchange, without being first converted into Bank of England notes, either by the drawer of a cheque, or by the party who is entitled to demand the payment of it.

When these obligations are so employed, they are, to all intents and purposes, notes payable on demand. Indeed, all that can be said of them may, with equal propriety, be predicated of a Bank of England note. A Bank of England note is one of the means of economizing the use of metallic money; that economy is a matter which concerns only the Bank of England. The possessor of a bank note is at liberty to exercise his pleasure and discretion as to whether he will receive, in the first instance, gold for his note, or pay away the note itself to another person.

It should be observed, however, that a large proportion of the deposits in the hands of the London bankers is not immediately required for the ordinary payments of the depositors. That part of his balance which is not immediately required by a depositor, and which is invested by the banker for his own benefit, is frequently described as dormant, or unemployed money. It is, in fact, employed and invested, although not on behalf of the depositor. That part which is drawn for, may be paid with bank notes, or it may continue in the form of a book debt of the same, or of some other banker, to some other depositor.

If this were merely a question of terms and of definition, it would hardly be worth while to dwell upon it. But there are some important considerations belonging to the question to which there will be occasion to advert hereafter. In the meanwhile, it may be useful to cite the following passages from M. de Sismondi's Principes d'Economie Politique, in which the economy of banks of deposit and of transfer, is clearly and correctly described.

"Les banques ont les premières donné l'idée du papier-monnaie, et l'invention elle-même des banques a été le fruit de combinaisons et d'observations successives. On saisira mieux peut-être et les raisonnemens et les illusions qui ont amené tant de peuples de nos jours à remplacer leur numéraire par du papier, si l'on commence par fixer son attention sur la manière dont une des plus anciennes villes de commerce de France faisait, avec un petit nombre d'écus, l'office d'un numéraire considérable.

"A Lyon, il était convenu dans le commerce, que tous les paiemens se feraient seulement à quatre époques fixes, qui, de trois mois en trois mois, suivaient des foires anciennement célèbres. Dans les trois jours que durait le paiement, toutes les affaires de la ville se soldaient ensemble. Chacun, à la même époque, avait beaucoup à recevoir et beaucoup à payer. Mais, dans les jours qui précédaient immédiatement le paiement, tous les marchands se rassemblaient à la Bourse pour faire ce qu'ils nommaient des *viremens;* c'est-à-dire, pour assigner réciproquement les uns sur les autres les sommes par lesquelles ils pouvaient solder leurs comptes. A devait à B, celui-ci à C, ce troisième à D, ce quatrième à E, et ce cinquième à A : par des viremens, tous ces comptes se trouvèrent soldés sans aucun paiement. Si cependant E ne devait rien à A, on chargeait A, par une suite de viremens de parties, de payer E ; et ce seul paiement acquittait les quatre comptes. Tous les marchands, n'achetant que pour revendre, ne reçoivent aussi que pour payer; et, si l'on voulait pousser jusqu'au bout les viremens qui peuvent se faire, on serait étonné de voir combien peu d'argent suffirait pour acquitter des affaires immenses.

" Mais toutes les dettes mutuelles ne sont point égales, et les appoints occasionent des difficultés et quelquefois des erreurs dans les viremens. L'invention des banques de compte y a suppléé. On en a vu quelques-unes se former d'une manière complétement indépendante pour le service des marchands qui voulaient se confier à elles. Le banquier n'était autre chose que le caissier des marchands ; il recevait et payait pour eux ; et, lorsqu'il faisait cet office pour un grand nombre de marchands à la fois, il arrivait le plus souvent qu'il se payait à luimême. Il n'avait point alors besoin de tenir morts dans sa caisse tous les fonds qu'elle était supposée contenir. Si, pour chaque centaine de 1,000 francs d'affaires qu'il faisait, il y en avait régulièrement 50,000 qu'il faisait avec lui-même, et dont le paiement s'effectuait en passant au crédit de B la somme qui était auparavant au crédit de A, il pouvait employer plus utilement ces 50,000 francs qui lui étaient inutiles pour ses paiemens : il faisait ainsi, avec la moitié moins de numéraire la circulation des marchands ses compatriotes, et il plaçait à intérêt l'autre moitié. En s'arrangeant pour avoir des rentrées promptes et faciles, à des échéances rapprochées, il était assuré de ne point faire attendre les demandeurs, lors même que, par extraordinaire, tous ses paiemens, pendant un certain temps, auraient dû se faire à d'autres qu'à lui.

" Plus un banquier étendait ses opérations, et plus il devait diminuer ses paiemens. Tous ceux que se font encore les soixante et dix banquiers de Londres, réciproquement, seraient supprimés si toutes leurs affaires se faisaient par une seule banque ; on jugea donc qu'il y aurait une grande épargne de numéraire et un grand bénéfice, à substituer une seule banque nationale de compte, aux divers banquiers. Ce fut comme un bureau ouvert pour faire constamment des viremens. Chaque négociant paya ou reçut, par une ligne qu'il fit écrire dans les livres de la banque, au débit ou au crédit de son compte, sans qu'il y eût aucun argent déboursé : entre négocians qui ont tous un crédit ouvert à la banque, l'opération du teneur de livres remplaça le plus facilement du monde celle du caissier, et aucune différence, ou d'appoint ou d'échéance, n'empêcha qu'on ne se transmît réciproquement des parties.

" Une banque de la nature de celle d'Amsterdam, ne sert qu'à ceux qui y ont un crédit ouvert. Beaucoup de négocians peuvent n'y pas avoir de compte, et tous ceux qui ne sont pas négocians, n'en ont presque jamais un, encore qu'ils soient appelés aussi à payer et à recevoir. Pour étendre jusqu'à eux l'économie des viremens, l'on inventa les banques à billets, ou de circulation, devenues ensuite si communes dans toute l'Europe.

" Jusqu'ici les banques n'avaient fait que simplifier les paiemens, épargner des transports inutiles de numéraire, et rendre la circulation facile avec une somme moindre qu'il n'aurait fallu sans elles. Mais quelqu'un devait profiter de ce qu'une moindre quantité de numéraire stérile était employée pour le commerce. Une partie d'un capital, qui auparavant ne portait point d'intérêt, pouvait être convertie en un capital fructifère, et quelqu'un devait en percevoir les fruits.

" A Londres, et partout où des banquiers se sont

établis pour être simplement les caissiers des commerçans, ces banquiers profitent de l'économie du numéraire qui en résulte, et c'est là le bénéfice de leur commerce."

Provincial Circulation.

Although the medium of interchange, in the provinces, consists, in a large proportion, of the gold and silver coin of the realm, and of the notes of the provincial bankers, payable, at the will of the holder, in coin, or in the notes of the Bank of England, yet the principal money transactions, as well between the inhabitants of the same town or district, as between different parts of the kingdom with each other, are liquidated by bills drawn upon the metropolis. London (it is observed by Mr. Henry Thornton) is, in this respect, to the whole island, what the centre of the city is to the suburbs. The traders who reside in the suburbs, carry on at home a variety of small payments, but their principal cash account is with the banker who resides in the heart of the city.

These transactions should naturally be liquidated by an internal circulation of bills drawn by one town or district upon another. But it is found more convenient to effect the liquidation by bills drawn upon, or made payable in, London. Liverpool draws upon London, in favour of Manchester; Manchester, in favour of Birmingham;

Birmingham, in favour of Leeds; Leeds, in favour of Liverpool. Of these bill transactions, a large proportion is effected through the medium of the country bankers, who give their own drafts upon London, or their promissory notes payable on demand, in exchange for the bills brought to them by their customers. The local notes are chiefly employed in the provincial districts in effecting the smaller payments. The larger transactions are liquidated in the manner above described, that is, with London money.

It has been questioned whether those alternations of prosperity and depression, of activity and dulness, in the state of the commerce and industry of this country, of which we have experienced so many remarkable instances, are mainly owing to sudden and unexpected changes in the channels of trade, or to something defective in the constitution, or erroneous in the management, of our banking institutions.

Mr. Norman, whose enlightened views and large experience entitle his opinions to the utmost attention and respect, observes, "The public in "general attribute much greater importance to "the fluctuations, and other causes, of our system "of currency, than they deserve. Nevertheless, "although sober reason denies the unfounded "assumption, that all great commercial convul- "sions may be traced to a faulty system of cur- "rency, there can be no doubt but that this "country has suffered greatly, of late years, from "the nature of its paper circulation." Mr. Loyd remarks, "The currency in which all transactions "are adjusted has the same reference to a healthy "state of trade, as the atmosphere in which we "all live has to the physical constitution of our "bodies: irregularities and disorders may arise "from a variety of causes, but the duration and "virulence of them will materially depend upon "the pure, healthy, and well regulated condition "of the medium in which they exist. A well "managed currency cannot prevent the occur- "rence of periods of excitement and depression, "nor of their necessary consequences, commercial "pressure and distress; but it may tend very "powerfully to diminish the frequency of their "return, to restrain the suddenness of their out- "break, and to limit the extent of their mischief." The prevailing opinion seems to be, that to whatever cause those alterations may be traced, the state and condition of the currency are materially affected by them; and that it is a matter of serious and lasting concern to enquire whether the banking establishments, by which a large portion of that currency is administered, are capable of being so controlled and regulated as to prevent, or at least to mitigate, the alarming consequences which we have so frequently experienced.

On this subject the following observations were written, but not published, in the year 1827.

"The great objection to a paper currency arises "from the extreme difficulty of subjecting its ex- "pansion and contraction to the same law as that "which regulates the expansion and contraction "of a currency purely metallic. It is obvious, that "in a country of which the currency is exclusively "metallic, and which possesses no mines of its "own, an increase or diminution of the quantity "of money can take place only through the "medium of its foreign trade. Now, as the pre- "cious metals are distributed amongst the com- "mercial nations of the world in such propor- "tions as to render the traffic carried on between "them purely a trade of barter, that increase or "diminution of money will naturally accommodate "itself to the traffic which would take place if "the precious metals had no existence. But is it "possible so to regulate an extensive paper cur- "rency as uniformly to preserve this level? What "criterion is there by which the issuers of paper "money can judge of its deficiency or its excess? "A demand for gold, and the state of the foreign "exchange? But all experience, especially that of "the last four years, has abundantly shown, that the

" intimations given by this criterion are often feeble " and uncertain; that the seeds of extensive mis- " chief may be planted and grow up long before any " distinct warning of coming danger is afforded " by it. The rate of interest? But this, although, " doubtless, a most important consideration in " the management and regulation of a paper cur- " rency, cannot always be exactly ascertained, " nor the changes to which it is liable, be dis- " tinctly foreseen. Besides, changes are con- " tinually being made by bankers in the nature " and kind of the securities upon which their " paper is issued. This, it has been said, is a " matter of no importance. It is, perhaps, of " none, when the change is completed; but " during the progress of the change it is of con- " siderable importance. If, during war, when " the income of the state is unequal to its expen- " diture, and the deficiency is to be made good " by loans, the Bank of England should, by " extending its issues, advance a considerable " part of the sum required, that increased quan- " tity of money will come into immediate contact " with commodities, elevate their prices, and de- " press the foreign exchange. If, during peace, " when the income of the state exceeds its expen- " diture, the bank should extend its circulation, " in order to enable government to redeem part " of the funded debt, a long period may elapse " before general prices are affected, and the "foreign exchange depressed. In the latter case, "the increased quantity of money does not, in "the first instance, act upon rude produce and "manufactured goods, but chiefly upon the public "funds, and securities bearing interest. In the "long run, however, general prices are affected. "Overtrading, and speculation in commodities, "fostered and encouraged by the abundance of "money, render a contraction of the currency "unavoidable, and universal consternation and "embarrassment ensue. Such is the process by "which, under the existing system, the Bank of "England is drained of its gold. The circula-"tion is unduly enlarged, and produces an unfa-"vourable exchange: the demand upon the bank "for gold for exportation occasions a diminution "of the quantity of bank notes: the contraction "of the London currency produces a similar "contraction of that of the country: an universal "panic ensues; and the bank then experiences a "further demand for gold to supply the deficiency "of the country circulation. The check given by "this process, to the fall of the foreign exchange, "being sometimes greater than the occasion re-"quires, is followed by a large, and long-con-"tinued, importation of gold, which it is not "always in the power, and, under such circum-"stances, hardly within the province, of the bank "to check. Then it is, when the value of the "currency is really raised above its proper value,

" we are told of the impossibility of maintaining, " under a heavy load of taxation, a currency " having gold for its basis, at the mint determina- " tion of £3. 17*s*. 10½*d*. per ounce. Such, in " many well-informed minds, is a prevailing " notion, at the present moment. An improving " revenue, and an increasing trade, will, it is pro- " bable, in no long time, compel those who have " formed this notion, to resort to some new expla- " nation of it.

" Are there, then, no means to be found, of " preventing those alternations of excitement and " depression—of extravagant expectation and dis- " appointed hope—but in the exclusive employ- " ment of so expensive a medium of interchange " as gold, and the suppression of paper ?

" The difficulty which this question implies, is " not insuperable. It is possible so to regulate " an extensive paper currency, convertible into " gold at the pleasure of the holder, as to render " its contraction and expansion, and the occa- " sional variation of its value, subject to the same " law as that which determines the expansion " and contraction of a currency wholly, and " exclusively, metallic."

Shortly after the foregoing observations were written, a memorandum, of which the following is a copy, was communicated to the late Mr. Huskisson :—

" The funds in possession of the Bank of

"England arise from three sources, namely, its "notes in circulation, the deposits of government "and of individuals, and its surplus, or undivided, "profits. Let it be supposed that these are as "follows:—

"Bank notes out -	£18,000,000	Securities - -	£18,000,000
"Public and private deposits - -	4,000,000	Bullion - -	8,000,000
"Undivided profits	4,000,000		
	£26,000,000		£26,000,000

"Although the foregoing statement may be "wide of the truth, it is sufficient to show that, "whatever may be the actual position of the "Bank, an increase or diminution of its cash and "bullion cannot take place without an increase or "diminution of its outstanding engagements, or "an increase or diminution of the profitable secu- "rities in its possession. If the latter remain "stationary, the expansion and contraction of its "liabilities will necessarily be accompanied by an "increase or diminution of its cash and bullion. "If the cash and bullion remain unaltered, its "outstanding liabilities will vary with the varying "amount of the productive securities.

"To the last-mentioned source of variation are "to be ascribed most of the evils which result "from a currency consisting largely of paper— "evils against which its convertibility into gold "is not always sufficient to guard.

"It is obvious that a country, of which the

" money is exclusively metallic, cannot experience " any augmentation or diminution of that money, " in any other way, than by exchanging com- " modities for money, or money for commodities, " with other countries. But when the Bank of " England increases or lessens its outstanding " paper, by an augmentation or diminution of its " advances upon securities bearing interest, no " extraordinary exchange of commodities for " money, or of money for commodities, with other " countries, necessarily takes place. The capital " and labour of the country remain unaltered, but " an artificial direction is given to both. The " effect thus produced, may be so slight as hardly " to be perceptible; but it is not therefore less " certain: some one or other is injured—uncon- " sciously, perhaps, but certainly injured—by the " change. It may be considerable; and when it " is so, a derangement of the national industry, " and extensive mischief, sooner or later, ensue.

" If the Bank of England were the sole issuer " of paper money, or if the country banks were, " in all cases, directly, and immediately, con- " trolled by the bank, the means of preventing " this source of unintended mischief, would be " obvious and easy. Nothing more would be " necessary than that the bank should con- " stantly hold a fixed amount of the same " unvarying species of securities. If its out- " standing liabilities amounted, at any parti-

" cular time, to £26,000,000., and if, against " these, it held £18,000,000. of government " securities, and £8,000,000. of bullion, then, " by confining itself to the £18,000,000. of " securities, the action of the foreign exchange " would necessarily turn upon the gold: at one " time the bank might have six, at another time, " ten, and at another, eight millions of treasure; " and in all cases, its paper would contract and " expand, according to the increase or diminution " of its bullion."

When this memorandum was written, it was seen and acknowledged that, however correct may be the principle contained in it, considerable difficulty would be experienced in its practical application. The principal difficulty, at that time contemplated, was the very fluctuating nature of the government deposits at the bank. It appears, however, by the evidence of Mr. Horsley Palmer and Mr. Norman, that about that period, or not long afterwards, the rule was adopted by the bank, although it has not, upon all occasions, been steadily adhered to.

It is now thought that the rule is insufficient for its purpose.

The main question, on this head, appears to be, whether the bank shall reduce the amount of its notes with every diminution of its specie reserve, or allow the public demand for gold to act at once on its notes, and its deposits.

In favour of the former rule, it is said that the bank should use its deposits as other bankers do theirs; and that its note circulation should be confined to a separate department — holding against the amount of notes outstanding, a fixed amount of securities, and a variable amount of bullion, and allowing the public to act upon the latter,—purchasing or receiving gold, when the exchanges are favourable to the country, selling or parting with it, when they are adverse. It is contended, that it is thus only that the circulating medium of the country, in so far as it depends upon the administration of the Bank of England, can be made to vary as it would do if it were wholly metallic; and, that in discharging the obligations which attach to its privilege of issuing paper money, the conduct of the bank ought to be so regulated as to produce this effect.

Such are the representations of those who call for a separation of the paper circulation of the bank from its deposit, or banking, business.

In order to establish the correctness and sufficiency of those representations, it would be necessary to show that the deposits of the bank essentially differ from its note circulation, and to point out the particulars in which the former so differ from the latter, as to act differently on prices, the rate of interest, and the foreign exchange. Unless this can be done, an objector may say, that by excluding the deposits from the effect of a demand for gold, whether originating in the wants of the provinces, or arising from an unfavourable balance of trade with other countries, we should not place things on the footing on which they would stand if the currency were wholly metallic; for if, when a demand for gold is made by persons drawing against deposits, the bank were to withdraw a corresponding amount of notes from circulation, it would contract the circulating medium, in a manner, and to an extent, that would not occur with a metallic currency. The objector may, moreover, say, that even if it be denied that deposits, under any circumstances, constitute a part of the circulating medium, still it must be admitted that a demand for gold, which, with a metallic currency, would operate, not to reduce the amount of coin circulating in the country, but only to withdraw a portion of that which is lodged in the coffers of the bank, ought not to be allowed to contract the paper currency to an extent which would not take place if the currency consisted solely of the precious metals.

These objections to a complete separation of the bank into two departments, cannot, I think, be altogether disregarded. We cannot absolutely exclude the deposits of the bank from the fund set apart to meet the demand for gold. Whether they should be altogether consolidated with the note circulation, is a separate question. To answer that question satisfactorily, we must acquire a clear notion of the nature of the various deposits at the bank, as contrasted with its note circulation. A statement from the bank, of those in its hands, classed under the three different heads of government deposits, bankers deposits, and drawing accounts—of the variations to which they are respectively subject—and in what manner, and to what extent, they are affected by a demand for, or an influx of, specie, would greatly conduce to the formation of correct notions on this head.

The manner in which a division of the business of the bank into two departments would probably operate, I endeavoured to explain in a paper which Mr. Tooke has done me the honour to insert in the third volume of his valuable work on prices; of which paper the following is a copy:—

"The rule adopted for the guidance of the "Bank of England in the management and "regulation of its liabilities, as explained by "Mr. Horsley Palmer and Mr. Norman, in their "evidence before the Parliamentary Committee "of 1832, is now supposed to be insufficient for "the attainment of the object proposed by it. "It is considered that a strict and inflexible "application of it to the joint liabilities of notes "and deposits would render it frequently ineffec-"tual, and sometimes injurious; that although "the deposits at the bank, and its outstanding

" notes, are alike payable in specie on demand, " yet only the latter affect the rate of interest and " the foreign exchange, and that a demand for " gold for exportation, or for domestic purposes, " or an influx of gold, in consequence of a favour- " able foreign exchange, may act only on the " deposits, without lessening or increasing the " amount of notes in circulation.

" In order to confine the rule to the promissory " notes of the bank, or, as they are usually " termed, its *circulation*, it has been proposed " that the business of the bank shall be separated " into two distinct departments, one to be called " the circulation department, the other the deposit " department: that the circulating department " shall hold a fixed and unvarying amount of " securities, and that its functions shall be con- " fined solely to the exchange of gold for notes, " and of notes for gold; and that the deposit " department shall manage the funds intrusted to " it, on the ordinary principles which are observed " by the London bankers, and independently of " the promissory note department.

" It may be worth while to inquire, what would " be the probable operation of such a plan.

" In carrying it into execution, I apprehend, " it would be proper, in the first instance, to " assign to the deposit department such a pro- " portion of the securities, and of the bullion, in " possession of the bank, as would, together, be

" equal to the amount of the deposits. Thus, if " the bank held eighteen millions of securities, " and nine millions of bullion, against eighteen " millions of outstanding notes, and nine millions " of deposits, it would probably be deemed ex- " pedient to assign to the deposit department six " millions of securities, and three millions of bul- " lion, and to retain in the circulating department " six millions of bullion, and twelve millions of " securities.

" If such a separation were made, it is obvious, " that as the exchange of gold for notes, or of " notes for gold, between the two branches, would " not affect the amount of bank paper in the " hands of the public, and as such interchange " might take place frequently, and to a great " extent, the increase or diminution of outstanding " notes would form no certain criterion of the " amount of paper circulating out of doors, unless " it were, at the same time, known what amount " of notes was held by the department of deposit.

" Disregarding, for the present, any objection " which it may be supposed would arise from this " consideration, let us at once proceed to inquire " what effect would be produced by a demand " upon the bank for bullion.

" The action and condition of the deposit de- " partment will be more distinctly perceived, if " we suppose that, under the circumstances above " stated, the whole of the three millions of bullion "are exchanged, on its first establishment, for "three millions of notes. The position of the two "departments would then be as follows:—

"*Circulating Department.*		*Deposit Department.*	
"Outstanding notes -	£21,000,000	Deposits - - -	£9,000,000
"Securities - -	£12,000,000	Securities - -	£6,000,000
"Bullion - -	9,000,000	Bank notes - -	3,000,000

"This being the position of the two depart-"ments, let us suppose that an adverse foreign "exchange has created a demand upon the bank "for bullion for exportation. Now, such a de-"mand for bullion may be satisfied, either by a "reduction of the notes in the hands of the public, "or by a reduction of the deposits at the bank. "If the former, then, the separation of the business "of the bank into two departments will have "answered the purpose expected from it; if the "latter, then, in so far as relates to the increase "or diminution of bank notes in the hands of the "public, by the action of the foreign exchange, "no satisfactory result will have been produced. "In the latter case, no advantage in the regula-"tion of the circulation will have resulted from "the separation.

"It may, perhaps, be said, that if the business "of banking were separated from that of circula-"tion, and conducted in the manner, and upon the "principles which are adopted by the private "bankers of the metropolis, a diminution of de-"posits would be immediately followed by the

" sale or realization of a corresponding amount " of securities, and thus the amount of bank notes, " in the external circulation, would be reduced to " an extent commensurate with the delivery of " bullion.

" But such a sale or realization of securities, in " similar circumstances, may be effected under the " present system of management. Whether the " existing system be continued, or the business of " the bank be separated into two departments, the " sale or realization of securities must depend on " the views and the discretion of the directors of " the bank. The only difference between the two " cases is this; that the counteracting effect occa- " sioned by paying out bank notes to the depositors " would be limited to three millions: upon the " present system it may be carried to a much " greater extent.

" It may be observed, moreover, that if the " demand for bullion for exportation should exceed " three millions, and if that demand should fall on " the deposit department, that department would " be reduced to the necessity, either of forcibly " realizing a portion of its securities, or of stopping " payment at a time when the circulating depart- " ment was abundantly provided with specie.

" It may be desirable to apply the foregoing " principles and observations to the actual position " of the bank, at certain periods, within the last " four years.

"In January, 1834, the liabilities and assets "were as follow:

"Circulation - -	£18,236,000	Securities - -	£23,596,000
"Deposits - -	13,101,000	Bullion - - -	9,948,000
"Rest - - -	2,207,000		
	£33,544,000		£33,544,000

"If, at that time, it had been determined to "divide the business of the bank into two depart- "ments, it would probably have been deemed ex- "pedient to assign £12,000,000. of the securities "to the circulating department, as a fixed amount "which was at no future time to be exceeded. "The remaining securities would, of course, go to "the banking department. The outstanding "notes, amounting to £18,236,000. would then "have for their basis £12,000,000. of securities, "and £6,236,000. of bullion. But, as the deposit "department would probably prefer notes to gold, "on account of the greater convenience of the "former, the position of the two departments "would have been as follows:

CIRCULATING DEPARTMENT.				BANKING DEPARTMENT.			
	Circulation.	Securities.	Bullion.		Deposits.	Securities.	Bank Notes.
Notes in the hands of the public - -	18,236			Deposits - -	13,101	—	—
Notes in the banking department - -	3,712			Rest - - -	2,207	11,596	3,712
	21,948	12,000	9,948		15,308		

The following would have been the position of two branches at the under-mentioned periods :

		Circulation.	Securities.	Bullion.			Deposits.	Securities.	Bank Notes.
1834 : Dec. Notes : Public - - -	18,304				Deposits	12,256			
Banking department	416	18,720	12,000	6,720	Rest -	2,522	14,778	14,362	416
1835 : July. Notes : Public - - -	18,283				Deposits	11,561			
Banking department	nil.	18,283	12,000	6,283	Rest -	2,644	14,205	14,244	nil.
1836 : Jan. Notes : Public - - -	17,262				Deposits	19,169			
Banking department	1,814	19,076	12,000	7,076	Rest -	2,599	21,768	19,954	1,814
Aug. Notes : Public - - -	18,061				Deposits	14,796			
Banking department	264	18,325	12,000	6,325	Rest -	2,813	17,609	17,345	264
1838 : Jan. Notes : Public - - -	17,900				Deposits	10,992			
Banking department	2,995	20,895	12,000	8,895	Rest -	2,609	13,601	10,606	2,995
1839 : Jan. Notes : Public - - -	18,201				Deposits	10,315			
Banking department	3,135	21,336	12,000	9,336	Rest -	2,500	12,815	9,680	3,135
July. Notes : Public - - -	18,049				Deposits	7,955			
Banking department	nil.	18,049	12,000	3,785	Rest -	2,686	10,641	12,905	nil.

"It will be seen, by the foregoing statement, "that if the business of the bank had been sepa- "rated into two departments, in January, 1834, "and if the rule, which we have supposed to have "been at that time established, had, since, been "inflexibly adhered to, the paper issues of the cir- "culating department, in July last, would have "been less by £2,364,000. than their actual "amount at that period, and the cash of the de- "posit department would have been wholly "exhausted. In July, 1835, and July, 1839, the "securities held by the deposit department would "have exceeded the aggregate amount of the rest "and the deposits. This excess of securities over "deposits this department could not have held, "unless the circulating department had trans- "gressed the prescribed rule to an extent equal to "the amount of that excess.

"In order to prevent the exhaustion of its cash, "the banking department would, no doubt, have "endeavoured to withdraw bank notes from the "hands of the public, by disposing of a large "amount of its securities. A rigid adherence to "the rule by the directors of the circulating "department, and a due regard to its safety by the "managers of the banking branch, would have "rendered the amount of the securities in posses- "sion of the latter, in July last, less by three or "four millions than it appears actually to have "been; or, which comes to the same thing, the

" amount of bank notes in the hands of the public " at that time would have been three or four mil- " lions less than it appears to have actually been. " The consequence would have been, a very severe " pressure on the money market.

" Hitherto, we have supposed the business of " the bank to be separated into two distinct de- " partments, and a formal apportionment of debts " and assets to have been made. Now, without " such a formal separation and apportionment, " precisely the same action upon the currency " would result from the strict observance of the " following rule ; namely, that the bank shall not, " upon any occasion, issue bank notes beyond a " certain amount (that amount we have supposed " to be £12,000,000.), except upon the deposit " of bullion. If this rule had been adopted in " January, 1839, and afterwards rigidly adhered " to, a great reduction of the securities held by " the bank would have been necessary, in order " to avoid a suspension of the payment of its " deposits. It is probable, indeed, that such a " reduction of the securities would have arrested " the drain of treasure at an early period of the " year. If, however, the drain had continued, " notwithstanding the reduction, it would have " been necessary, in July last, to have carried the " reduction to the extent of three or four millions " below the amount which the bank actually held " at that period.

"It may here be proper to observe, that the "difference between the rule above mentioned "and that explained by Mr. Horsley Palmer and "Mr. Norman, in their evidence, is this;—that, "while the former rule would preclude the bank "from issuing notes in the payment of deposits "to a greater extent than is equal, in amount, to "the difference between the amount of notes at "any time outstanding and £12,000,000. plus the "amount of bullion in possession of the bank, the "latter would allow the bank to substitute notes "for deposits to an unlimited extent. The former "rule would be the same in its operation as a "division of the bank into two departments. The "sole effect of the latter would be, the increase or "diminution of the aggregate amount of the notes "and deposits of the bank with the increase or "diminution of its bullion.

"Whether a formal separation of the bank into "two departments take place, or the rule last "mentioned be adopted, it may be expected that "the public will be exposed to very great alterna-"tions of comparative ease and difficulty in the "operations of the money market.

"There is one point connected with the pro-"posed division of the bank into two departments "to which I have not adverted, but which it may "be material to notice. It has been suggested, "that, in order to increase the disposable funds of "the banking department, it would be desirable

" that a certain portion of the capital of the bank " now lent to the state, should be made available " for banking purposes. By this I apprehend it " is meant, that a portion of the three per cent. " stock in which the original capital of the bank is " invested shall be sold, and the proceeds of the " sale invested in other securities, and in commer- " cial loans and discounts, at the pleasure and " discretion of the bank.

" Of this suggestion it may be observed, that it " is a proposal to withdraw a certain amount of " funds from the use and employment of one " class of persons, in order that it may be trans- " ferred by the bank to the use and employment " of another class of persons. By this process " no new funds would be created in the money " market. The change would be merely the " transfer of funds already existing from one kind " of investment to another. The operation would " be the same as that of an individual stockholder " who sells his stock in order to employ the money " arising from the sale in commercial discounts. " The operation of the individual stockholder " would, in its consequences, be comparatively of " little importance; but if five millions of the " original capital of the bank were sold, as has " been proposed, and the proceeds of the sale " mixed up with and employed in the same " manner as the deposits at the bank, although " no greater reserve of bank notes in the banking

" department, in consequence of this accession of " funds, would be necessary, yet the varying em- " ployment of funds of such magnitude, during " alternate periods of commercial excitement and " depression, might produce a prodigious effect " upon the general circulation. At one time the " additional fund might be employed in commer- " cial loans and discounts; at another time a " great part of it might be withdrawn from the " public, and held by the bank, in bank notes and " specie; thus creating an alternate abundance " and scarcity of money in the hands of the public, " at the pleasure of the bank."

If it should be determined to adopt the proposed plan of separation, the most difficult, and by far the most important, point for consideration, would be, to determine the fixed amount of securities to be held by the department of issue. If that point were once properly settled, the principal object of the plan might be attained, without a formal division into two departments, of the business of the bank. Such a separation would be desirable only as it might afford a better security than could be otherwise obtained, that the fixed amount of securities would, at no future time, nor upon any occasion, however urgent, be exceeded.

In the supposed case above stated, namely, that previous to the separation, the bank is in possession of £18,000,000. of securities, and £9,000,000.

of treasure, against £18,000,000. of outstanding notes, and £9,000,000. of deposits, I have assumed the fixed amount of securities, to be held by the department of issue, to be £12,000,000. If that were the amount fixed, the outstanding notes must, according to the prescribed rule, be £21,000,000., of which, as £18,000,000. are supposed to be in the hands of the public, £3,000,000. must necessarily be placed at the disposal of the banking department.

In a letter to Mr. Tooke, lately published, Colonel Torrens has assumed, for the purpose of illustration, the same supposed case, and has fixed the amount of securities to be held by the circulating department, at £9,000,000. In so fixing the amount, he places (under the circumstances supposed) the banking department precisely in the situation, the possibility of which is contemplated by Mr. Tooke, that is, that of being without either notes or gold, wherewith to pay any immediate demands of the depositors, and of being obliged, in order to obtain the requisite means, to force on the money market the sale of a portion of its securities. He supposes that, for this purpose, a sale of £3,000,000. of securities would be necessary, and that, consequently, the £18,000,000. previously in the hands of the public, would be reduced to £15,000,000.

Notwithstanding this pressure on the money market, we are to suppose that an adverse exchange has produced a demand upon the bank for gold to the extent of £3,000,000. Colonel Torrens then says, "The £3,000,000. bank notes, held by "the deposit department, as reserve, would be "drawn out by the depositors, and paid into the "circulating department, in exchange for gold; "while the directors of the deposit department, "in order to recover a reserve equal to one-third "of their deposits, would be obliged to sell "£2,000,000. of the £6,000,000. held in securities. "The results would be, that in the circulating "department, the bullion would be reduced from "£9,000,000. to £6,000,000., and the circulation "from £18,000,000. to £15,000,000.; and that "in the deposit department, the deposits would "be reduced from £9,000,000. to £6,000,000.; "the securities from £6,000,000. to £4,000,000.; "and the reserve from £3,000,000. to £2,000,000. "It is self-evident that the effect would be, not "only a contraction of the circulation, but a limi-"tation of the power to overtrade in discounts and "loans."

To reduce the amount of bank notes in the hands of the public, from £18,000,000. to £13,000,000., would, indeed, effectually prevent overtrading in discounts and loans.

Although so extreme a case as that put by Colonel Torrens is not likely to occur, yet if it were to occur, all the consequences which he has described would ensue, without a separation of debts and assets, from a strict observance of the rule described in the paper communicated to Mr. Tooke, namely, that the bank shall not, upon any occasion, issue notes beyond a certain fixed amount, except upon receiving into its possession a corresponding amount of gold. A division of the business of the bank into two departments, or a strict observance of the rule, without the division, would produce the same results.

There is one material circumstance, however, which renders it doubtful whether a separation of functions in the way proposed, would be the most effectual means of obtaining the requisite security for the due observance of the rule.

Hitherto it has been the practice of the Bank of England to cancel all notes brought in for payment,—never to re-issue them. Now, although an adherence to this practice would not occasion any insuperable difficulty in carrying out the proposed arrangement, yet it would render it necessary that the banking department should generally keep on hand a very large amount of gold, or of notes signed, and ready for delivery. To hold a very large amount of notes signed and completely executed, might be deemed hazardous or inconvenient. If, in order to avoid that risk and inconvenience, the banking department were to keep on hand the cancelled notes, and require from the department of issue new notes for the old ones, at such times, and to such an extent, as suited its occasional wants and convenience, the department of issue would be virtually a depository for the banking department, and, through the banking department, a depository, to a greater or less extent, for others. Arrangements might, no doubt, be made, and a system of checks contrived, that would prevent any violation of the principle of the plan; but the requisite machinery would be a matter of considerable nicety, of which the operation and the object would not easily be perceived and understood by the public.

There is another important consideration which should be noticed.

It may be questioned whether the rule could with justice and propriety be applied to the Bank of England without being, at the same time, extended to all the banks of issue in the kingdom.

To extend the rule to all banks of issue, and to ensure a strict observance of it, would be a work of almost insuperable difficulty. It would, in effect, be to determine that the note circulation of the whole kingdom, payable on demand, shall be confined to a limited amount, except upon the deposit of bullion; and that the privilege of issuing that limited amount shall be divided amongst the different bankers, in all the towns and districts of the kingdom, in certain proportions, to be determined by persons appointed for that purpose.

Rather than submit to a restriction of this nature, it is probable that most of the provincial bankers would use only the notes of the Bank of England; in which case, it would be a matter for serious consideration whether it would not be better at once to determine that the paper circulation for the whole kingdom shall be confined to a single issuing body. Indeed it would probably be found, that this would be the only means of effectually carrying out the principle of the measure. If, however, it should be determined to confine the issues of paper to a single corporation, and if that corporation were the Bank of England, the difficulty of determining the proper amount beyond which the bank shall not issue notes, except upon the deposit of bullion, would be very greatly increased.

The principal object aimed at by the advocates for a separation of banking functions, and the confinement of the issues of paper money to a single central body, is the prevention of such a fall in the value of the money of this country, relatively to that of other countries, as might endanger the convertibility of the paper: in other words, such a depression of the foreign exchange as might, on the existing system, drain the Bank of England of the whole of its specie reserve.

If the amount of securities to be held by the deposit department were fixed sufficiently low, this object would, in all probability, be accomplished. All the paper in circulation beyond that amount, whether held by the deposit department of the bank, or in the hands of the public, would consist of notes for which there would be a corresponding amount of gold lodged in the coffers of the bank.

To determine the fixed amount of securities, then, is the sole essential point which the scheme involves; the rest is merely matter of account and book-keeping.

It is supposed, that these measures, if adopted, would render the paper circulations of the kingdom subject to no greater fluctuation in amount and value than those to which a currency exclusively metallic is liable.

Now it may be observed that, whatever may be the *amount* of the paper, so long as it is promptly convertible into gold, at the pleasure of the holder, its value, and that of the gold coin which it promises to pay, must, in London, be exactly the same.

To what fluctuations the value of our mixed currency of paper and gold is liable, relatively to the currencies of other countries, is a separate question, which it is of importance to consider.

The prevailing opinion seems to be, that the value of the currency of this country, relatively to that of other countries, is affected by the fluctuations of foreign trade, and depends on the amount of foreign payments; that a large and unusual importation of foreign corn, or the necessity, from whatever cause arising, of effecting an

For Product Safety Concerns and Information please contact our EU representative GPSR@taylorandfrancis.com
Taylor & Francis Verlag GmbH, Kaufingerstraße 24, 80331 München, Germany

www.ingramcontent.com/pod-product-compliance
Lightning Source LLC
LaVergne TN
LVHW021110300926
849160LV00009B/666